THE VERSATILE MILLSTONE
WORKHORSE OF MANY INDUSTRIES

by

Jon A. Sass

SOCIETY FOR THE PRESERVATION OF OLD MILLS

Published and distributed by:

Society for the Preservation of Old Mills
604 Ensley Drive, Route 29
Knoxville, Tennessee 37920
U.S.A.

Library of Congress Cataloging in Publication Data

Sass, Jon A.
    The versatile millstone workhorse of many industries.

    Includes index
    1. Millstones--History.   I. Title.
TS2149.S27   1984   664'.7203'028   84-13839

ISBN   0-930497-00-7

Printed and bound in the United States of America

PREFACE

With this volume **The Society For The Preservation of Old Mills** expands its publishing activities beyond that of the quarterly magazine, *OLD MILL NEWS,* to the occasional presentation of important individual works which significantly contribute to a better understanding of Molinology. It is the Society's belief that this and future works will be important additions to American technical literature.

Paul Flory, until retiring, was an active miller and mill owner. In his *OLD MILL NEWS* articles he has shared many experiences, but until now we have not had an in depth examination of the results of his avocation - collecting millstones. His collection, which was located at his home in Martic Forge until being divided between The Smithsonian Institution and Flowerdew Plantation, was certainly the most extensive in America – extensive not only in number but also in the many various uses represented.

John Sass is an Englishman we had the good fortune to have with us in the United States for several years. It is American Molinology's loss that he has returned home for we were assured many studied works such as this one from him in the future. From his work at Flowerdew Windmill, articles in *OLD MILL NEWS,* and these pages, it is apparent that Mr. Sass has keen understanding and insight concerning the subject of millstones and their uses.

While it will become clear to the reader that stones were once common parts of the technology of many industrial processes, there has been very little scholarly documentation of this in the past. It is, therefore, appropriate for the Society to publish this fine introduction to an important subject.

TABLE OF CONTENTS

FOREWORD

Much has been written about the mill both in a nostalgic and architectural vein, but relatively little is written about the heart of the traditional mill - the millstone. A few period textbooks include advice about the best form of dress, speed and composition of millstones, but these are now long out of print, difficult to come by, and on the whole, address themselves specifically to the flour miller.

Upon taking up the position of Curator of Molinology and resident miller at the fine post windmill in operation at Flowerdew Hundred in Prince George County, Virginia, one of my tasks was to catalog more than eighty millstones and grindstones. These stones had been acquired from Mr. Paul B. Flory on the disposal of his impressive collection at his home in Martic Forge, Lancaster County, Pennsylvania. Through subsequent contact with Mr. Flory, I realized how diversified and important the original collection had been.

The aim of researching and compiling this booklet is to allow the reader to gain some small appreciation of the great variation of form and use to which our forefathers put millstones. I hope it may be of interest to both the general reader and the student of molinology, and will also further stimulate study and recording on the subject of millstones before it is too late.

Jon Antony Sass
Grovewood
Brigg Rd.
Hibaldstow
S. Humberside DN20 9PD
England

The Windmill at Flowerdew Hundred
Prince George County, Virginia

ACKNOWLEDGEMENTS

Mr. and Mrs. David A. Harrison III, of Flowerdew Hundred Farm, Prince George Co., Virginia, for their interest in purchasing and preserving a large portion of the Paul B. Flory Collection of millstones which are to be formally displayed and interpreted at Flowerdew Farm to compliment the fine windmill they commissioned to be erected.

The Flowerdew Hundred Foundation, Hopewell, Virginia, for access to their collection of former Flory millstones and photographs of same; also for the opportunity to study in depth and research the background material of these millstones.

Mr. Paul Flory for his many kindnesses, and allowing me access to his catalogs and accumulated notes on his millstone collection, trade catalogs and photographs.

To the Society for the Preservation of Old Mills and especially Michael LaForest, Editor and Publisher of **Old Mill News,** for his encouragements and efforts in enabling this paper to be published.

Armstrong World Industries Inc. Armstrong Cork Divisions, Lancaster, Pennsylvania, and in particular Mr. C. E. Sawyer, Assistant Plant Manager, Lancaster Plant, for production information.

Mr. Arthur D. Dunn, Ottawa, Canada, for obtaining analysis on the composition of certain of the millstones.

The Hershey Chocolate Company, Hershey, Pennsylvania, and in particular Mr. Robert H. Schock, vice president manufacturing, for information on chocolate production.

Mr. Charles Howell, North Tarrytown, New York, for his advice and information, particularly in the field of stonedressing.

The Smithsonian Institution, The National Museum of American History, and in particular Dr. G. Terry Sharrer, Assistant Curator of Division of Extractive Industries for prints and details of the former Flory millstones in their possession.

Dr. Carter Litchfield, for details of hemp mill technology.

And last but not least, my wife, Anne, for typing the text.

INTRODUCTION

Before Paul Flory's important private collection was broken up in 1973, it was possibly the largest and most diversified assemblage of grinding and crushing stones on display in the U.S.A.

Paul Bowman Flory was born in 1898, the third generation of a milling family with mills still operating in Lancaster County, Pennsylvania. His absorbing hobby began in 1930 when workmen at the mill, then owned by Flory and his brother Jacob, were preparing to remove and dump two long discarded millstones. He had them hauled to his home in Martic Forge where they formed the nucleus of his eventual exhibit of over 230 stones ranging from a primitive Indian mortar and pestle to a flint grinding mill comprised of four stones with a combined weight of nearly eight tons.

Before long, acquaintances in the milling fraternity were offering him redundant stones, and as his interest grew he began to search out unusual and rare examples of stone being utilized for many varied industries.

In pursuing his quest for interesting additions to his collection he was instrumental in salvaging and preserving some durable chunks of America's fast disappearing industrial heritage. If it were not for his zeal many of these artifacts would have been lost forever. Through diligent research he was able to trace the history, function and origin of most of his "proteges."

Over the years, he was also able to acquire some unusual additions from fellow collectors and Charles Ross and Son Company a mill furnishing firm formerly in Brooklyn, New York. Mr. Flory learned of the Ross Collection in 1955. They were the remnant stock in trade of that firm when they abandoned stone mill manufacturing between the two World Wars. Unfortunately, Mr. Flory was unable to extract any details of the manufacture or the particular functions of some of the more unusual stones. Some were in the condition they were received from the quarries near Esopus in New York State; some were partially dressed, and others marked out for dressing but not worked upon. In 1965, the business moved its premises to Long Island and Mr. Flory was able to acquire the remaining stock of nearly 100 stones.

The early grain mills of Colonial North America were predominantly equipped with millstones imported from Europe. Popular ones being French Burrs, Cullen or Blue Stones from Germany, and English stones of millstone grit.[1] Native American stones were used increasingly from the mid 18th Century for practical and economic reasons. The main factor was the scarcity and cost of stones imported from Britain following the Revolutionary War and the War of 1812. As new frontiers were opened up further west and the cost and hardships of transporting heavy stones from the east coast increased, suitable local rock was tried particularly for grinding the staple crop of Indian corn, or maize.

European millstones were represented by examples of all three popular stones mentioned above. French burrs, quarried in the area of La Ferte sous Jourarre and Epernon in the Paris Basin, have long been renowned for their outstanding quality in enabling white flour to be extracted from wheat. French millstones are recorded as being imported into Virginia as early as 1620.[2] Examples in the collection show various combinations of marrying the different blocks or panes of burr into a completed millstone. Combinations vary from one with six "keystones" radiating from the eye to the skirt, to another with eighteen blocks forming two concentric rings with the "white" harder and close textured pieces forming the outer ring and the more porous softer burrs forming the inner ring. In the early years of colonization, the completed millstones were imported from Europe, but by the early 19th Century several American French-stone makers were in business in the major ports and milling centers. Some had their own agents supervising the selection of burrs in the French quarries.[3]

Cullin or blue stones have been quarried and mined around Andernach on the Rhine in Germany at least as early as the Roman occupation of that area. They derived their name from a corruption of Cologne, the main distribution center for those millstones. They were once popular along the Eastern seaboard of U.S.A. and worn out examples can be found at many old mill sites.

Millstones known to British millers as Peak or Grey stones were quarried and hewn out of millstone grit found in thick layers in parts of the Pennines, the "Backbone of England". There remains to this day large numbers of both completed and unfinished millstones in the extensive quarries around Hathersage, west of Sheffield in the heart of the English Peak district. These stones were popular in Britain for grinding grain for animal feedstuffs and making wholemeal flour long before the colonies were set up along the eastern shore of North America and so it was only natural that the millers in the English colonies would import these well proven stones into their adopted country. This same view might be assumed for the other European settlers and those other proven European stones mentioned above.

Native American stones are represented in the collection by granite and a variety of conglomerates including Cocalico and Esopus Stones. Millstone quarries are recorded in Virginia as early as the 1750's.[4] Possibly, records will come to light recording even earlier quarries elsewhere. Although the better flour mills retained French burrs for producing high quality wheat flour, many rural mills used locally hewn stone particularly for making cornmeal from maize and for grinding animal foodstuffs.

Cocalico stones are so named because they were hewn from the pink and tan pebbly conglomerate stone around the township of Cocalico in Lancaster County, Pennsylvania. They were monolithic and usually banded with iron hoops. As with other native American stones, sometimes cast iron balance weights were trapped between the circumference of the stone and the iron bands. The conglomerate varied from very small to large pebbles. The stones were used extensively in Pennsylvania for grinding corn (maize).[5]

Esopus, or 'Soper' (Yankee) stones were first quarried at High Falls in Ulster County, New York State, at a location known as Traps. They are made out of a single piece of light gray to white Shawangunk Conglomerate grit and again banded as the Cocalico stones to prevent shattering in operation caused by fault lines in the stone. The main quarrying and shipping center was Esopus about ten miles south of Kingston on the banks of the Hudson River. Many of the Esopus stones in the Flory Collection came from the Ross Manufacturing Company's stock.

The granite stones in the collection came from a number of locations such as Maryland, New England, Rhode Island, New Hampshire and Rowan County in North Carolina. The latter is still used as a source by the Meadows Mill Company.[6]

Many of the American horizontal mill stones had a flat, unfinished surface on the non-grinding face. This face was sometimes left rough, but was often capped with plaster of Paris or mortar to help balance the stones. Usually, balancing was assisted by lead or iron weights let into the capping. The plaster backing also enabled the runner stone to be swept clean from time to time. The capped stones were often used for grinding meal for human consumption and can be confused with French burr stones when viewed encased in the millstone furniture.

Some of the older horizontal runner stones in the collection had been cut to receive the fixed four arm rynd. Some of these were converted and certainly the later stones were carried by and balanced on the normal two arm balance rynd with the driving iron socketed at right angles to this in the usual North American practice.

Millstones are generally thought of in the context of grinding grains and seeds. But particularly before the advent of mass produced steel and its alloys in the latter half of the 19th Century, stone crushers and grinders were employed in a most varied range of industrial uses from crushing ore to extract minerals, to crushing apples for cider. Over the centuries man learned by experience that certain rocks were better suited for reducing specific materials and different applications of the millstones and designs of mills were evolved.

By the late 19th Century many sophisticated stone mills were offered for sale by manufacturers who had developed into specialized businesses. The millstone and the technology of grinding and crushing had at last become a science rather than an art. While the best pattern of dressing a working face of a millstone was now arrived at by scientific deduction and exhaustive testing, some of the patterns of dress held in high regard by the craftsmen of earlier centuries were now held to be a barbarism. The various forms of circular dress (not to be mistaken with the older sickle dress) and logrithmic dress, for example, replaced the less efficient straight quarter dress with the varying draft circles of its subordinate furrows.

Stone mills have held their own against the encroachment of steel attrition and roller mills in certain fields. For certain applications, they are still considered superior. Coffee beans and spices, paints and color pigment, for instance, are still ground extensively by stone. Other industries have only in the last decade or so reluctantly discarded these time tried work horses. An increasing demand by the health food market has caused a resurgence of stone ground grains in recent years and many an old mill has had a new breath of life blown into it by a loving owner to meet this discerning market.

---

[1]For further details on Peak millstone industry read *Peak Millstones and Hallamshire Grindstones*, by Jeffrey Radley, MA. excerpts of transactions of Newcomen Society, Vol. XXXVI, pages 165-173, 1963-4.

[2]"Two French millstones sent in the ship 'Supply' which left England in September 1620 bound for Berkeley Hundred" (On the James River, Virginia) adapted from a list in Smith of Nibley papers and is available in published form in the Bulletin of New York Public Library III, No. 7. (July 1899) pages 283-290 also in the Records of Virginia Company of London Vol III, pages 385-393. It cannot be deduced however whether the above are French burr stones or merely millstones from France.
Also purchased and on the Supply:-
20 Bushells of wheat at 3s. 6d.
9 Bushells of 3 square wheat in ears in 2 great pipes at 4s.
4 Milpecks (picks or chisels for dressing millstones).

[3]Trade advertisements from the late 18th Century onward cite millstone builders manufacturing French millstones from imported burr blocks. e.g. 1774 James Webb, Little Queen Street on the North River, New York City. Well known firm of Munson and Hart (later Munson) of Utica, NY. Established 1825.

[4]"David Laird 300 acres including ye millstone Quarry at ye foot of ye Peaked Mountain near Divers Land July 29, 1758". From entry book of Thomas Lewis, *County Surveyor* recorded in Virginia Magazine of History and Biography Vol. 31, page 245. Old Peaked Mtn. Church is at Cross Keys Rockingham County, Virginia.

[5]For further details of cutting Cocalico stones see *Old Millstones* paper read by Paul B. Flory to the Lancaster County Historical Society, Pennsylvania. Vol. LV, 1951, No. 3.

[6]Meadows Mill Company, North Wilkesboro, North Carolina. Reputedly last company still manufacturing natural stone mills in U.S.A. Millstones ranging in size from 8" to 30".

[7]Thomas Jefferson refers to the adoption of balance rynds in preference to older fixed rynds in a letter of 1787 as though it was a recent innovation. *Thomas Jefferson's Farm Book,* page 345.

MORTAR and PESTLE

The pounding of wild grain, berries or nuts between two stones to create a more digestable food source probably pre-dates *Homo sapiens.* Certainly, simple pounding stones gradually evolving into mortar and pestle have been found throughout the world by archaeologists and are still in use today by some primitive societies. A handsomely carved mortar was discovered on the site of the Chaldean Royal Palace of Tello and has been tentatively dated at 4,000 B.C. - a relic from the dawn of civilization in the Middle East.[1]

The mortar and pestle in the Flory Collection was retrieved from the Cocalico Indian Settlement in Pennsylvania. Examples hollowed out of boulders or more often shaped out of hard-woods were common among the many native American tribes. The portable wooden mortar and pestle was a particularly valuable asset in the nomadic lifestyle of many of these Indians and fine specimens are displayed in a number of Museums of American History. They were sometimes adopted by the pioneer European settlers when the more advanced rotary hand querns were unobtainable or uneconomical to small outlying communities. They were also extensively used during the Colonial period for the making of hominy.[2]

In the area of Cocalico Township, Lancaster County, Pennsylvania, many large boulders of local red sandstone had been sculptured by nature to form "water bowls". Continuous pounding of grain with pestles of suitable natural stone gradually increased the dimensions of these hollows forming excellent mortars and were particularly suited for grinding the flint varieties of maize.

The naturally formed thin cylindrical pestle found in the close vicinity of the sandstone mortar is of a rock not found in the geology of Lancaster County.[3] It is therefore likely that it was obtained as a trade item by the local inhabitants bartering with a distant tribe. This form of barter is recorded in relation to other stone implements and materials for such necessities as arrow and spear points.

This mortar and pestle from the Flory Collection weighs 450 pounds. The base measures 30" x 17", and the pestle measures 2" x 8". The stones were used by American Indians, probably of the Susquehannock tribe, during the 18th or early 19th century. Moss is seen growing around the lip of the mortar.

1

In the absence of documents it can only be assumed that the mortar and pestle slowly evolved from the primitive pounding stones. Continuous pounding of a hand held stone would eventually form a cavity in the bed stone, particularly if it was of a soft nature. It must have been appreciated that grain in this hollow cavity scattered less under impact than on a flat surface. As the mortar evolved into its classic form, the trade mark of the apothecary, a longer pestle had to be fashioned to work in the deeper recess.

The mortar and pestle with its mainly pounding or impact crushing could not be evolved further and was surpassed by the saddle stone and its decendents which introduced rubbing, shearing and pressure crushing to grain milling. The impact principle of reduction was taken up by other industries in the form of stamp mills and ball mills. Vegetable dyes including indigo were pulverized by special forms of mortars and pestles.[5] Stamp, and more recently ball mills, have been used with great success in crushing rocks and mineral ores for many years.[6]

The ball mill is receiving renewed attention in the grain milling field and is also used in some forms of middling purifiers where a small cylinder is rotated slowly so that the balls tumble gently on the middlings and separate the flour from the bran particles. Another form of mill - the hammer mill with its rotating arms which strike and crush the grain until the meal is fine enough to pass through a screen - has met with wide acclaim in the feed industry.

---

[1]Discovered by French explorer M. De Sarzec and described by him in a paper read before the Academie Des Inscriptions et Belles Lettre in 1894. See also *History of Cornmilling,* Vol. 1, by Bennett and Elton, reprint 1898 edition by B. Franklin, New York, 1964, page 88.

[2]Originally an American Indian dish of maize (or Indian corn) hulled and ground more or less coarsely and prepared for food by being boiled with water or milk.

[3]Information on stone pestle given by the late Dr. Herbert M. Beck of F. & M. College Lancaster, Pennsylvania.

[4]*Bulletin de la Societe d'Encouragement pour l'Industrie Nationale,* 7:170-174, with plate showing the indigo mill of Le Fevre (Paris, 1808).

[5]For example, the water wheel driven snuff mill at Sharrow, Sheffield, England, and elsewhere.

[6]Referred to again later in this study and Gypsum mills.

SADDLESTONE OR METATE

The saddlestone derives its name from the analogy that the concave upper surface of the bedstone compares to the seat of a saddle. Consistant use formed and increased the concavity. On this surface grain was rubbed and ground by a small stone "muller" pushed back and forth by hand.

The saddlestone evolved from crude crushing and grinding stones and has a distinguished place in the story of millstones as it was one of the first contrivances by which grain could be made into meal by a true grinding action rather than pounding and crushing. It is still in common use in places as far apart as Central and South America, Africa and India. Examples of saddlestones have been recovered from many prehistoric sites in Europe, and the Middle East. Small models and statuettes depicting the stones in use by slaves have been found in several royal tombs of ancient Egypt. Wall paintings in the 5th dynasty tomb of Ti, 2,600 B.C. show milling and baking scenes including several saddlestones and mortar and pestles in use.[1]

The ancient civilizations of Mexico and Central America produced great numbers of saddlestones some of which were superbly crafted with handsome ornamentation and often standing on carved legs. The saddlestone is known in the new World as the *metate,* derived from the Aztec word *metlatl.* The smaller hand held cylindrical or flat rubbing stone is known as the *mano* (Spanish for hand.)

The example in the Flory Collection was a cruder device from the Hopi Indian Reservation in Arizona. It was used by Pueblo Indians to grind the softer and floury varieties of maize grown in southwestern United States.

The *metate* if not of bedrock, was sometimes set on the ground or propped up at a slight angle in a small bin made of wood or flat stones on edge. The grain to be ground was either dried and separated from the cob, or in some areas, was treated to first remove the grain hulls (pericarps).[2] This treatment was much favored in the New World, and originated somewhere in Mexico or Central America. It was achieved by boiling the grain with leached wood ashes (lye) or quicklime, and later washing off this alkalai and the softened and loosened hulls. This disposed of the problem of having to separate the flakes of the hull (or bran) normally created in grinding before a good sample of meal could be achieved. The grain was first bruised and then ground by the action of the *mano* being pushed back and forth.

Throughout history the tedious task of operating the saddlestone and the mortar and pestle was invariably set aside for women or slaves. An observer in Sudan noted that a female slave was expected to grind enough meal sufficient for one day's consumption for eight people if she worked from morning to evening.[3] The finer specimen of saddlestone will produce meal of reasonable quality making use of the natural abrasive nature of the stone; saddlestones rarely having any dressing.

---

[1] Storck and Teague, *Flour for Man's Bread,* (Minneapolis, 1952), p. 67. See also Bennett and Elton, *History of Corn Milling,* Vol. 1, Chapter 11.

[2] Paul Weatherwax, *Indian Corn in Old America,* (Macmillan Co., New York, 1954), p. 94.

[3] Werne, *Source of the White Nile,* (London, 1841), p. 142.

THE QUERN

The rotary quern is the direct ancestor of the larger millstone still in use. The millstone declined in popularity following the widespread adoption of the roller milling process in the 1870's.[1]

Somewhere among the ancient civilizations bordering the Eastern Mediterranean evolved the concept of grinding grain between a rotating upper (runner) stone and stationary lower (bed) stone. The first attempts were no doubt crude but still a definite improvement, both in quality of meal produced and reduced effort involved, over the mortar and saddlestone methods.

Gradually, the quern as we know it evolved with a hole or eye through the axis of the runner stone to feed grain down onto the grinding faces. A spindle carried and balanced the runner bearing on a bar, or rynd, let into the eye of the stone. A handle secured to the runner enabled it to revolve with relative ease. Later, simple tentering devices ensured the two stones were kept slightly apart preventing grit rubbing off the stones and contaminating the meal.

The Romans were conversant with the quern and another form of rotary mill known as the *mola versatilis*. This Roman mill is known commonly as an hour-glass mill with a runner stone shaped like a hollow hour glass running on a conical stone bed. Some fine examples of these were discovered when a bakery in Roman Pompeii was cleared of ash from that fateful eruption of Vesuvius in 79 A.D. The *mola versatilis* was recorded as early as the second century B.C. and could be large and elaborate enough to require the services of an ass or a number of slaves to turn them.

Many of the Roman hand querns had a form of dressing on their grinding faces similar to the 'quarter dressing' of later millstones. This is no doubt developed from early experiments with the saddlestone and its more refined adaption, the pushmill, where grooves or furrows were sometimes cut into the grinding surfaces of the stones as they crossed each other. This added a shearing action to supplement the natural abrasive quality of a stone.[2] The use of the quern spread throughout the Roman Empire and gradually to the rest of the Old World.

The quern is the antecedent of the successful horizontal millstone.

The native Americans who came into contact with the European settlers also realized the great advance in technology from the mortars and *metates* and before long were imitating the European examples. Specimens of both European and Indian adaptions of the hand quern are displayed in several museums interpreting early Americana.

The fine example in Mr. Flory's possession is, he maintains, "the best find in my 50 years in which I handled nearly 300 millstones". He and his wife have frequently produced excellent corn meal with it for their own consumption.

The quern was fashioned by the Seminole Indians of Florida. The stones were hewn out of coquina rock[3] and were so expertly fashioned that they varied in circumference by only an eighth of an inch. The stones are mounted within a hollowed out cypress log. A wooden bar wedged across the 4″ diameter eye of the runner stone pivots and carries the stone mounted on a wooden spindle. The spindle passes through a hardwood bush in the center of the bedstone and bears on a bridge tree at its lower end. The bridgetree, privoted at one end, can be raised or lowered by a wedge to give the desired gap between the millstones. Grain is fed into the eye of the runner stone by hand and is ground by the natural abrasiveness of the two undressed stones. The top stone revolved by means of a long handle protruding above the stone and fitted into a socket cut in the stone's skirt. For long periods of operation the combined effort of two people standing opposite one another worked the mill.

----

[1]Mills using rollers in place of traditional millstones were originally developed by Jakob Sulzberger in Hungary (1834). By 1873, Fredrick Wegmann's designs had greatly improved the roller milling process. From then on, and with further improvements, the roller mill was adopted as the standard plant for merchant flour mills. (See also, Storck & Teague's, *Flour for Man's Bread.*

[2]L. A. Moritz, *Grain Mills and Flour in Classical Antiquity,* (Oxford Clarendon Press, 1958), p. 37-49. Fig. 5.

[3]A sedimentary rock comprised of limestone saturated with fossilized sea shells.

EDGE RUNNER MILL

This is probably the oldest example in the Flory collection of a mill powered by sources of energy other than human endeavor.

The mill consists of a base or basin stone made out of one piece of limestone approximately seven feet in diameter in which a heavy, bevelled edge runner stone was rolled round by an ox or other draft animal. A stone plinth protruding above the trough in the center of the base stone has a stout vertical pivot post securely wedged in a socket to form an axis around which the edge runner traveled. The edge runner has a horizontal wooden axle passing through its axis secured in place by iron rings and tapered keys. The oxen would be yoked and connected to this shaft. A wrought iron collar encompassing the vertical axis and secured to the horizontal driving shaft ensures the runner stone follows a constant circular path.

The mill was reputedly used to crush grain presumably having a similar action to the current smaller roller mills found in farms and rural mills to provide rolled oats for animal feed.

Mr. Flory was informed by the farmer who previously owned the mill that the grain was spread in the path of the runner stone, about a bushel at a time, then when the crushing and attrition action of the revolving stone was completed the resulting "meal" was removed by broom and shovel and a new charge was added. The mill was probably shared by many settlers in the vicinity in the days before the numerous and more efficient watermills appeared in that area. This mill was retained in use well into the 19th Century by the farmer for producing feedstuffs as it saved him the time consuming and arduous task of carrying relatively small amounts of grain over difficult terrain to the local custom mill.

This type of edge runner mill has been in use since long before the birth of Christ and adapted for many tasks from crushing mineral ores to cider making.

The oxen-powered grain mill with edge runner formerly of the Algar Shirk farm, W. Cocalico Township, Lancaster Co., PA. (Photo courtesy of the Smithsonian Institution).

THRESHING AND HULLING STONES

Threshing in its primitive form was either achieved by human endeavor and the wooden flail which was a tedious, tiring and dusty task, little relished by our farmer forefathers, or accomplished by draft animals "treading the grain".[1] Ancient civilizations frequently used cattle to "tread out" the grain spread out on a prepared threshing floor. Both oxen and horses were used in rural North America on many larger farms until the invention of practical threshing drums in the late 18th and early 19th Century revolutionized this time consuming task.[2] Obviously, treading the grain was neither efficient or hygienic, the threshed grain suffering from animal pollution!

The Egyptians are known to have used their *charatz* which was like the "stone boat" still used on Eastern farms for gathering field stones. It was left rough on the underside and dragged over the threshing floor usually by oxen. The Hebrews had a *Moreg* - a sled like frame with spiked cylinders between the runners - that revolved upon the grain as the implement was drawn around. Similar devices were known to the Romans which they called the *traha* and *tribulum*. Devices of this nature are still to be found in use in the Eastern Mediterranean and elsewhere today.[3]

One of the more common methods of threshing in rural Asia is still by stone rollers -- their circumference deeply corrugated or fluted. They were frequently supported in a wooden frame and hauled over the threshing floor or were rigged up in a similar fashion to the edge runner of the oxen mill, already described, and drawn around the circular threshing floor by the draft animal.[4]

Hulling or shelling stones were used for removing the husk or hulls from cereal grains such as barley, oats, rice and buckwheat. The principle by which the grains are hulled is that of rubbing them against one another between the working faces of the stones with great force so that they hull one another without being much crushed or broken by the stones. The hulled grain discharged from the stones usually fell into a sieving device where the dust and dirt was separated from the hulled grain and then the lighter husk and chaff were blown off with a fan. In some of the early mills the process was repeated through more than one pair of stones - this was so in mills cleaning and polishing rice.[5]

---

[1] Referred to in Deuteronomy 25:4. "Thou shalt not muzzle the ox when he treadeth out the corn."

[2] J. T. Schlebecker, *Whereby We Thrive*, pp. 32-33. Two men and six horses could thresh about 100 bushels a day or about six acres of wheat. For details of treading floors etc. see *Thomas Jefferson's Farm Book*, (University Press of Virginia, 1976), p. 77. *The Grain Harvesters* by Graeme R. Quick and Wesley F. Buchele has good coverage and illustrations depicting the development of threshing and threshing machines.

[3] Quick and Buchele.

[4] *Ibid.*, Includes illustration of wooden variations usd in U.S.A. and Europe. Also, Rudolf P. Hommel, *China at Work*, pp. 73-76.

[5] Oliver Evans, *The Young Millwright and Miller's Guide*, (New York, 1972), pp. 251-253. (13th Edition, 1850, Reprinted by Arno Press). *China at Work* by Rudolf P. Hommel gives illustrations of Chinese examples of wooden and clay-faced rice hulling millstones. Small hand operated querns were used in colonial North America for hulling rice. Examples are in the Mercer Collection, Doylestown, Pennsylvania.

ROLLER TYPE THRESHING STONE

This device was brought to the U.S.A. by members of a sect of Russian Mennonites. Some of these hard working, devoutly religious farmers eventually settled in Kansas in the 1860's bringing with them other primitive and outmoded farming equipment. It is significant that the United States taught the newly settled Menonite farmers much about advanced technology in farming implements, and that these former Russsian farmers in return brought the best seed to take the greatest advantage of that technology. It was these Menonites that introduced "Turkey Red" wheat into Marion and Harvey counties, Kansas, in 1874 from which the world renowned North American hard red winter wheats were developed.[1]

The star shaped hewn block of limestone having the appearance of a seven toothed spur gear was reluctantly sold by a Mennonite farmer in McPherson County, Kansas in 1957 where it had be relegated to the corner of a field for more than 75 years. It is an example of the older form of threshing stone being "tumbled" by hand. Other examples still to be seen in Kansas were later drilled partly (or wholly) through their axis to allow stub axles to be fitted so that they may be drawn by either man or beast.

Threshing stone -- This Russian Mennonite threshing stone is from McPherson County, Kansas. The stone was rolled over a packed earth floor to release small grains after reaping. (Photo courtesy of the Smithsonian Institution).

"I have personally 'tumbled' the stone on a level surface", recalled Mr. Flory, "and was surprised to learn the small amount of energy needed to do so for it was standing on only two of the seven ridges. To upset or turn it was very easy".

These threshing stones were tumbled by hand or drawn by one or two horses over loosely spread grain attached to the reaped stalks on a threshing floor previously prepared. This floor was created by clearing a piece of ground roughly circular in shape, mixing the soil with chaff and water until a plaster like constituency then rolling and smoothing when dry. The sun baked surface was then hard enough to stand the punishment of threshing.

After threshing, the straw would be lightly raked off and the released grain gathered up and winnowed to remove the loose husks and pieces of straw.

The roller thresher stones were formerly commonly found in Eastern Europe through Asia. Sometimes the smooth-faced roller used to level the threshing floor was also used to thresh the grain. But more often, the face was corrugated or fluted the length of the roller. Occasionally, the roller was in the form of a frustum of a cone laid on its side so that it would more easily be dragged in a circular path over the spread sheaves.[2]

---

[1]K. S. Quisenberry and L. P. Heitz, "Turkey Wheat: The Cornerstone of an Empire," in *Agricultural History* Vol. XLVIII, No. 1, (Agricultural History Society, 1974).

[2]Quick and Buchele, p. 42. Also, Hommel, pp. 75-76.

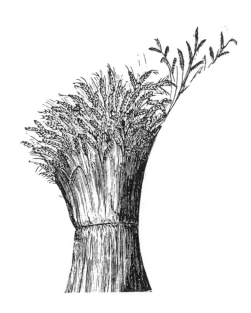

CLOVER SEED CLEANING MILLS

Red clover, noted for its quick growth, was imported from England into North America during the 18th Century and was highly regarded as a herbage for fodder, and for its reviving properties when turned in to improve and reclaim exhausted soils. After cleaning, the surplus seed was often sold to dealers in Philadelphia and other commercial centers.

When grown for its seed, the clover was harvested when mature with a horsedrawn clover header. The tops of the dry clover were traditionally trodden by horses on the threshing floors of the commodious Pennsylvania barns. Smaller quantities were flailed by hand to separate the seed from the pod. Both processes created a great deal of obnoxious dust harmful to the lungs of both man and horse.

By the 1820's, millers in the premier clover growing area in Pennsylvania (Chester and Lancaster Counties) were pioneering the cleaning of clover seed by mills. The earlier mills had horizontal runner stones usually four feet in diameter and were powered to rotate at approximately 100-120 rpm. The runner stone had a large eye, often 14 inches diameter, to allow free access of the seed pods and adhering stems that had been removed from the rest of the plant by prior flailing or treading. The stones, particularly the runner, were given a 2 inch hollow bosum and a true face of only 5 - 7 inches of the outer skirt of the circumference. The skirt had no furrows in either stone, but was picked rough with a pritchell to create sufficient friction as was necessary to free the chaff from the seed. In this form it was similar to the traditional wheat and oat hulling stones. Needless to state, much attention was paid to set the stones perfectly level and the gap between the working faces set far enough apart so as not to crush or damage the seed, but close enough to clean it.[1]

An improved version of the stone clover seed mill had a cone shaped under runner. This is the type of millstone found in the Flory Collection and others in Pennsylvania.[2] The under runner, like the upper runner in the mill already described, was normally carried on a fixed three or four arm rynd. The face of the stone took the form of a very flat cone with a raised boss in the center, and dressed with coarse, wide, screw-like furrows which drew the soft chaffy clover down onto the outer half of the stone. This work face was either picked roughly with a pritchell, or dressed with shallow, narrow furrows of straight quarter dressing. Other examples had straight, equal length furrows, radiating from the center. Occasionally, sickle dressing was found.

The fixed cover stone had a large eye like the earlier mills and large enough to encompass the boss of the lower stone. The dressing on the working face was usually of straight furrows about one eighth of an inch deep radiating from the center forming a slightly ribbed face which helped rasp and turn the seeds as they passed through the mill.

Descriptions exist of the layout and operation of these mills. The mill was ideally of two or more stories to facilitate the storage of the clover seed and to house the fanning and elevating machinery also needed in the cleaning process. It was advised that the stones be mounted on a stout hurst frame set about twenty inches below the level of the ground floor so the stones ran immediately below that floor. The cover was removable so that a stone crane could be swung over to dismantle the stones for periodic dressing and cleaning. The wide eye of the upper stone prevented choking by the chaffy seed. The under runner mill had the great advantage here in not having the constriction of the rynd or driving bar of an upper runner.

Clover seed cleaning stones from a Pennsylvania mill showing the cone-shaped underrunner and fixed upper stone. (Photo courtesy of the Smithsonian Institution).

Seed fell from the stones into the trough of a bucket elevator and was carried to a fanning machine in the upper floor where it fell through a coarse vibrating screen, or riddle, which separates the straw from the seed. The dust and loose chaff was blown outside through a pipe which measured the full width of the fan and approximately sixteen inches deep. The seed and chaff which fell through the coarse riddle was returned back to the stones for a second cleaning. The seed was then elevated to a second smaller fan about half the size of the first where it fell onto a shaking sieve of fine brass wire. The process was continued until the particular parcel of seed was considered clean enough. It was recommended that a small waterwheel should power the fans with a belt drive independent from the main mill drive to ensure even running of the fans. A fan with insufficient draft could choke the machinery, while too much draft could cause the light seed to be blown out of the mill with the separated chaff and dust.

The cleaning of clover seed was considered a winter time occupation best carried out in cold dry weather when up to ten or twelve bushels a day could be cleaned in ideal conditions. Many mills were opened up in the clover growing area of Pennsylvania each providing a custom service to local farmers within a five or six mile radius and charging a toll of ten percent for the service rendered. Early reports recommended millers with weak lungs to avoid the business![4] It must have been far worse for farmhands threshing the clover or supervising the treading by horses and then winnowing the poorly separated seed in a barn!

Clover seed threshing and cleaning machines improved throughout the 19th Century making the dirty, tedious and time consuming earlier process obsolete. A report of 1835 stated that a strong laborer could ply the flail from morn 'til night and be thought to have done a good day's work if he cleaned about 15 lbs. of seed.[5] On the other hand, by the 1890's, a combined clover seed thresher, huller and cleaner could produce 10 or 12 bushels an hour![6]

---

[1]Calib Kirk, *American Farmer,* Vol. II, No. 42, Jan. 12, 1821, pp. 335-336 and Vol. II, No. 45, Feb. 2, 1821, pp. 357-358, Brandywine, Pennsylvania.

[2]*The Musselman Millstone Collection,* Ephrata, Lancaster Co., Pennsylvania, The Mercer Collection, Doylestown, Bucks Co., Pennsylvania.

[3]Kirk, Vol. II, No. 42, pp. 335-36.

[4]*Ibid.*

[5]S. Edward Todd, *Report of the Commissioner of Agriculture,* "Improved Farm Implements" (U.S. Department of Agriculture, 1866), pp. 225-288.

[6]A. J. Pieters, "Seed Selling, Seed Growing and Seed Testing", Improvements in harvesting and cleaning grass and clover seeds, pp. 565-566. *1899 Yearbook of U.S. Department of Agriculture,* (Pub. 1900), pp. 549-574.

OAT SHELLING MILLS

Oatmeal manufacture was relatively little known and practiced in the U.S. although practiced to some extent in Canada.[1] In North West Europe including the British Isles, there were formerly many smaller mills producing the coarsely ground meal which was known as groats in Britain.

A prerequisite of milling oats was the drying and then shelling of the grains. The majority of oat mills had a drying kiln. This was very necessary in the damper climate where oat cultivation was generally carried out. Drying enabled the outer shells and dusty down, which envelopes the kernels, to be more easily removed in the shelling process.

Shelling stones were best made from a coarse, even textured, moderately soft sandstone. Those quarried in the vicinity of Newcastle, England, had the highest reputation.[2] Millstone grit, from the English Pennines and elsewhere was also popular. Shelling stones were usually of similar diameter to conventional horizontal millstones but not as thick and heavy since shelling requires little pressure.

The bedstone face was usually perfectly flat while the runner stone often had a bosum of about 3/16" (5mm) running out to nothing at about two-thirds of its diameter. The outer third was faced flat and true like the bedstone. Shelling was best performed by stones that were as sharp and rough as possible. To achieve this both stones were normally picked rough with a pritchell and had no furrows. The runner stone was traditionally mounted on a fixed three or four armed rynd, and the gap was maintained between the two grinding faces equal to the average length of an oat kernel.

Centrifugal force of the runner stone, unaided by furrows, impelled the grains through the stones. A higher rate of feed through the eye than would be expected in conventional grinding caused the grains to bombard one another. The passage of each kernel was further impeded by those in advance of it and those tumbling over it from behind. In this environment, the shells were split off the kernels and the downs dust shaken off as the grains somersaulted and jostled to the skirt of the stone. Fastidious millers ran the oats through the shelling stones twice. The first time the runner was set higher than the second which tended to shell cleaner and produce less broken grain and waste.

The end product issuing from the shelling stones passed over a shaking screen of fine wire which separated the dust and meal from the kernels and the shells were then extracted through a winnowing fan which delivered the kernels clean and ready for grinding into groats.

The older stones were usually of four to six feet diameter (1.22m - 1.82m), and sometimes served the dual purpose of shelling and grinding on a rerun by reducing the gap between the stones. When this was the case, the runner stones often had a few lead furrows which assisted the outward movement of the oats and groats. The pair of stones in the Flory Collection, reputedly imported into Pennsylvania from England *circa* 1740, have such a dress. The runner stone has four evenly spaced furrows with little draft radiating out from the eye effectively dividing the face into four quarters or harps. The lands of the runner and the face of the bestone was picked all over with a pritchell. Because the dry shelled kernels required little pressure to grind them into the coarse rounded groats, preferred by tradition and for improved keeping properties, the larger older diameter stones needed only a small grinding surface. This was achieved by bosuming or in some cases by enlarging the eye. Examples

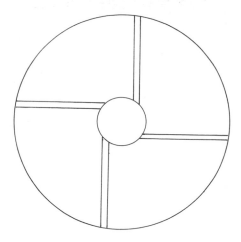

An oat shelling stone for removing the husks from oats. The face between the furrows may be picked over with a pritchell. The original stone is in the custody of the Smithsonian Institution, Washington, DC. (Drawing by the author).

with eyes of 22″ (55.88cm) are known. In the latter example, there was a bosum 1/4″ (6.35mm) deep at the eye tapering out to a true face at two thirds of the radius. This left the center third to effectively granulate the kernels. These large stones were difficult to keep on 'an even keel' and had to have the spindle trammed frequently to maintain an even gap between the faces of the stones. Because of this, stones during the 19th Century were reduced to diameters of 42″-48″ (1.06m - 1.22m) for shelling, and as little as 28″-36″ for grinding the groats. The diminished size of stone involved a corresponding reduction of eye and bosum and of course less power to drive the runners.[3]

As with other traditional types of millstones the dress varied from the norm. Oat stones with scroll dressing similar to the buckwheat hullers, and other patterns, are known. Later in the 19th Century, shelling stones made of wood faced with an emery composition became available which would no doubt retain a sharp face and stand the friction of shelling.

Following the shelling process, groats were frequently made using millstones having conventional grain milling dress. Great care was needed in the attention to feed and tentering of the stones. The groats were then sifted. The conventional sifter generally had three sieves of tin or galvanized tin punched with round holes of suitable size and spaced a few inches apart one above the other in a frame with each sieving tray having an outlet for the bran at one end.

---

[1]David Craik, *Practical American Millwright and Miller,* 1870, p. 353.
[2]*Ibid.,* p. 356.
[3]*Ibid.,* p. 361. Craik maintained that the power to drive both the oat shelling and grinding stones together with necessary cleaning and sifting apparatus and elevators would be about the same as that required for one pair of flour or cornmeal stones.

BUCKWHEAT HULLING STONES

Buckwheat takes its name from the Dutch "Bockweit" and the German "Buchweize" or beech wheat and is so called because the seeds resemble both in shape and color the triquestrous beech nut. It was introduced into Europe from its native Central Asia by the Turks in the 13th Century. In Western Europe, buckwheat is grown primarily to provide animal feed. Formerly, buckwheat groats also provided an inexpensive staple food particularly before potatoes became widely accepted. The groats were usually cooked to make a gruel or porridge and a semolina type pudding. Colonial settlers introduced buckwheat and groat mill technology into their adopted homeland of Eastern North America.

The normal prerequisite for groat manufacture required the buckwheat to be roasted in a kiln. This, as with oats, loosened the hard outer shells or hulls enabling them to be more easily removed by the hulling stones. After roasting, and prior to grinding, the buckwheat was passed through a sifter with multiple sieves to remove any loose shells and dust. The groat or hulling mill served a similar function to oat shelling stones, shelling and coarsely grinding the buckwheat. The hulled and cracked grains that issued from the stones are known as grits. These grits passed through another sifter and were further cleaned and graded. Finally, the various grades were purified of remaining hulls and dust by being passed through several groat machines. They were similar to a winnowing machine comprising of a simple casing with an internal fan.

The examples of buckwheat hulling and groat millstones in the Flory Collection were all found in Pennsylvania and are representative of the technology of former mills in Germany and the Low Countries where buckwheat groat mills were common until at least the mid 19th Century.[1] These stones were all approximately three feet in diameter. The runner stones were carried on three armed fixed rynds which socketed in recessed iron castings leaded into the eye of the stone. The stone could be leveled on the rynd by set studs threaded through the three feet of the eye castings.

Buckwheat Hulling Stone -- This buckwheat hulling stone is from McCrabbs Mill, Drumore Township, Pennsylvania. The subsidiary furrows have a curvature equivalent to the millstones radius drawn from center lines on each of the eight master furrows.

A runner stone of millstone grit has four straight master furrows radiating from the center of the eye (no draught) effectively dividing the working faces into quarters. The remaining curved furrows radiate at right angles from the master furrows. The arc of these furrows is equal to twice the overall diameter of the stone. One bedstone has eight quarters (or harps) divided by eight straight master furrows. Curved subsidiary furrows radiate from these master furrows; their arcs are based on the radius of the millstone. The convex back of the stone has four cut outs set equidistant around the circumference to locate adjusting screws or wedges and align the stone on its frame. Leveling of the bedstone is the first essential requirement in setting up any pair of millstones to run sweetly and in balance. Over the centuries many devices, patent and makeshift, were adopted to achieve this.

Another pair of stones of quartz conglomerate found at Freys Mill near Alinda, Spring Township, Perry County, Pennsylvania, have a scroll like dressing. The arc of a master furrow is equal to the radius of the stone. The arc of a subsidiary furrow is equal to a quarter of the stones radius.

The empirical, trial and error kind of dressing of the above stones exemplifies, in the author's experience, how experimentation through the ages has decided the best pattern of dressing - even if unorthodox - to provide adequate distribution of the material being processed and to carry out the particular type of reduction required of various materials using differing types of stone and motive power.

Buckwheat was also ground into meal for making pancakes, cakes and muffins. The buckwheat was again hulled through the type of mills already described and then ground into meal using a conventional pair of millstones usually having a sickle dress. The meal was then passed through bolters (dressers) to remove all traces of husk. Animal feed was coarsely ground through a further pair of stones in a one step process.

---

[1]A good example of a complete horse powered groat mill complex can be inspected at the Netherlands Open Air Museum at Arnhem, Holland.

This buckwheat hulling stone has four master furrows. The arcs of the subsidiary furrows are drawn on circles having radii equal to twice the diameter of the millstone.

BARLEY PEARLING MILL

The barley pearling mill removed the hulls and the tough bran which covers barley grains, leaving the kernels clean and white -- the pearls. Wheat treated in a similar fashion was the basic ingredient in a nurishing traditional dish called frumenty (a favorite of the Author).[1] In the north of England and Scotland these two products were often given away by millers to their customers and landlords as a gift at Christmas.

In its usual form, the mill consisted of a wide circular stone, mounted horizontally like a grindstone, surrounded by a casing of perforated iron sheeting. The type of rock most suitable for pearling should be a sharp, coarse, even textured sandstone similar to that used for oat shelling stones. The 19th Century examples known to the author ranged in size from smaller stones of 36 inches (91.44cm) diameter by 15½ inches (39.37cm) wide, to the largest 60 inches (152.4cm) diameter by 10 inches (25.4cm) wide. The best results were obtained from mills having stones of smaller diameters and wider faces. These were also safer in operation. Examples offered by British mill furnishers as late as the 1920's had stones ranging from 28 inches (71.12cm) to 36 inches (91.44cm) in diameter, and from 10½ inches (26.67cm) to 18 inches (45.72cm) wide.[2] The stone was carried on an iron spindle and was normally secured by cast iron blocks and keyway, or was leaded to the spindle which itself ran on bearings mounted on a sturdy timber frame. The perforated iron sheets surrounding the stone were screwed and nailed to a strong wooden frame work. This cage or drum was constructed in halves to allow adequate access to the stone for dressing or replacement.

Ideally, a new mill was constructed as to provide a gap of approximately 1 inch (2.54cm) between the circumference of the stone and the perforated iron casing, and approximately ¾ inch (1.90cm) at the side. This gap would of course get greater as the stone wore and was redressed. Some stones were picked all over with a pritchell similar to the oat shelling stones already described. Some stones were cracked or stitched with a chisel. The cracks formed lines across the stone on its circumference and from these lines to the eye on each side. Long practice and observation, however, proved that stones with good abrasive qualities did not require such dressing and only required checking periodically when any high spots taken down and glazing removed. The iron sheets in the older mills were usually perforated with a round or square pointed punch from the outside leaving the burrs protruding inwards like a grater. The better mills of the latter half of the 19th Century were punched with holes approximately ⅜ inch long (0.95cm). The rows and individual holes all being equally spaced. Some mills had only the circumference of the casing perforated, others had the sides perforated also. The theory was that the extra side perforations would quicken the pearling process and provide extra ventilation to cool the stone and barley which became heated due to friction.

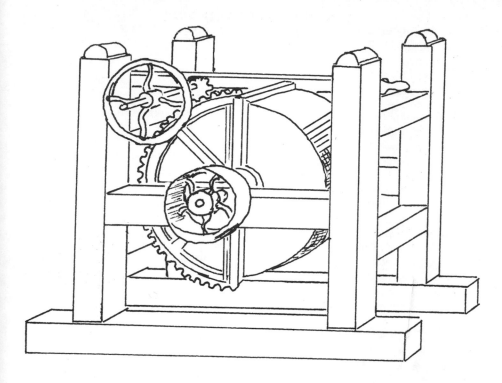

A typical barley pearling mill in which the pearling was done between the adjacent faces of the perforated iron cage enclosing and slowly rotating in the same direction as the horizontally mounted, and quicker revolving, central stone.

A small hinged door in the circumference of the drum allowed a charge of barley to completely fill the gap between the casing and stone. The drum had to be sufficiently strong to prevent bursting if the mill became clogged during operation. The mill usually operated in the following manner with a few minor variations. A flat pulley on one end of the stone spindle transmitted power through a belt to rotate the smaller diameter stones at about 500 rpms. Rotation was correspondingly less for larger stones where the danger of the stone shattering increased with dire consequences to operator and mill.[3] The drum was designed to revolve at a much slower rate than the stone, and usually in the same direction of rotation as the stone.[4] One method of driving the drum can be observed in this chapter where spur gear segments secured to one side of the casing's circumference are driven from a flat belt pulley and pinion. The drive to the drum can be disengaged by a slide lever drawing the pinion out of mesh with the spur gear.

When the drive was applied to the mill, frequently using jockey pulley to tighten the slack belts, the hard outer hulls were gradually rasped off the barley kernels by the abrasive stone and burrs of the perforated drum. The separated hulls also assisted in scouring away the thin, tough cuticle which shrouds the kernels inside the hulls. If the stone was too heavily dressed the kernels would be cut up too much, rounded, and wasted away. Similarly, if the barley was not kept tightly packed the kernels could be worn to the size and shape of a small white pea before the seam in the side of the kernels were properly cleaned out. To prevent this, the drive to the drum was disengaged with the slide lever once or twice during the making of one batch. Partially pearled barley, kept on hand for the purpose, was packed in the space left as dust and hulls were ejected from the mill through the perforations.

A batch of pearled barley could be made in about twenty minutes using a mill with a stone 37 inches (93.98cm) diameter by 15 inches (38.1cm) wide.[5] When the operator, through repeated sampling, judged that the process was complete the pearled barley was let out the mill, and it was fed slowly through a sifter comprising of up to four different mesh grade screens. This removed the dust and shattered pieces and further separated the barley into different sizes. The hulls were then blown off by a fan.

The pearling mill could also be used as a primitive smutter to remove the obnoxious fungus dust from small grain by the simple expedient of rotating the drum only with the drive to the stone disengaged.

----

[1]Frumenty (frumety or furmety) - A dish made of hulled wheat boiled in milk and seasoned with cinnamon and sugar.

[2]Examples quoted from trade catalog circa 1925 of William Garner and Sons, 72 Mark Land, London, England.

[3]David Craik, *Practical American Millwright and Miller,* (Philadelphia, 1870). Describes some accidents with pearl barley machines due to operator negligence in allowing the mill to run empty.

[4]Author has recorded mills operating with outer casing revolving at velocity of between one and two feet per second.

[5]Craik, p. 376-7. Mills set up for Mr. John McKenzie of Burke, New York, 1860's.

MILLS FOR MAKING SPLIT PEAS

The making of hulled, split peas is closely allied to the business of producing oatmeal and pearl barley. The trade was little known in the United States but more common at one time in Northwestern Europe.

The peas were first soaked in a bath of cold or slightly tepid water. This moistened and swelled the farinose berry of the pea and caused the more impervious oily hulls to loosen and burst. The peas were then spread out to drain the excess water and finally dried in a kiln. Where peas were processed in the same building as oats, the kiln was normally used for peas immediately after clearing a batch of oats while the kiln was still warm. However, the remaining fire was removed to avoid smoke discoloring and tainting the peas. The oat shelling stones would then be set further apart to remove the hulls which would later be fanned off.

In America (and possibly in Europe) where peas were processed other than in an oatmeal mill, different forms of mills were sometimes used which were also used for hulling buckwheat. One can occasionally come across discarded stones from these mills.

One type of split pea mill was comprised of a stone in the shape of a frustum of a cone which could be rotated on its axis within a jacket or thick ring of similar stone. This outer jacket was usually girded with iron bands to prevent shattering. The mating surfaces of both stones were picked all over with a pritchell like the lands of an oat shelling stone. The peas passed between these two faces as the stone cone revolved. The gap between the faces could be adjusted by raising or lowering the cone on its axis. During the 19th Century, this form of mill was superseded by a mill of similar shape and principle of operation but constructed of heavy perforated sheet iron.

Another mill used for splitting peas and hulling buckwheat comprised of a stone similar in appearance and operation to the stone in a pearling mill. Underneath was slung a concave piece of stone which resembled the outer trough of a grindstone. This concave stone enclosing approximately one quarter or more of the circular stones circumference was hung in an adjustable frame. The spring loaded adjusters allowed the concave to be set closer or more distant from the revolving stone, and allowed it to yield to any foreign material passing through the mill.

The circumference of the center stone and the adjacent face of the concave were both dressed with shallow grooves forming "V" shaped patterns. The "V's" of the center stone were cut with the open ends of their triangle facing forward in the direction of rotation. Those in the concave were cut in the opposite direction. The patterns resembled those of the teeth in a helical gear.

The draft caused by the rotating stone drew the peas in at the top of the trough and threw them out split at the other end. The "V" shaped dressing gathered the peas towards the center of the path and threw them out in a round stream onto a sieve which caught the peas while passing the smaller trash. A small fan then blew off the hulls, and peas were ready for marketing.

The accompanying pictures of shelling mill runners and a jacket for the runners are taken from the Musselman Collection, Ephrata, Lancaster County, Pennsylvania.

The central stone cone and outer mating cylinder from a pea splitting and hulling mill. Stones are found in the Musselman Collection, Ephrata, Lancaster County, PA. (Photo courtesy of Dr. Carter Litchfield).

WHEAT CHAFF STONES

A pair of two foot diameter wheat chaff stones each cut out of a single piece of pebble conglomerate rock were found discarded in the attic of a typical, small and old-established custom grist mill in Pennsylvania operating one pair of millstones.

The stones were used as a preliminary cleaning stage before wheat was ground into flour in the days when threshing by wooden flail and "animal treading" was in vogue. They appear to have been used before the innovation of improved winnowing fans such as the Dutch fans c. 1770's, and the mechanical threshers, whose use became more widespread and improved after the turn of the 19th Century.[1] Thomas Jefferson was recorded as having a pair of stone "rubbers" for cleaning the grain in his custom mill.[2]

When wheat was threshed by flail or "trodden" by animals, a certain amount of chaff remained adhered to the grains. The threshed grain was fed into the eye of the runner stone. The stones were not dressed in the conventional manner with furrows and lands, but the working surfaces were pocked, with a pritchell. The runner had to be well balanced. Through centrifugal force the chaff was removed from the grains as they rolled and rubbed against one another on their passage to the circumference. The treated grain was then tossed in a winnowing basket or tray to remove the separated chaff and other unwanted material. The stones were housed in a conventional wooden casing or vat. Those in the Flory Collection had been driven by water power but could no doubt be worked on a farm by an animal gin. The pair of stones, now in the care of the Smithsonian Institute, are a rare survival of this obsolete and tedious method of cleaning grain.

---

[1]Schlebecker, p. 33. Also, Quick and Buchele, Chapters 6 and 7.
[2]*Thomas Jefferson's Farm Book,* p. 403.

Wheat chaff stones found in the dismantled Habecker Mill, Lancaster County, Manor Township, Pennsylvania. (Photo courtesy of the Smithsonian Institution).

CONE SHAPED UNDER RUNNER MILLS

The principle of enabling gravity to assist in the movement of grain between the working surfaces of millstones was early appreciated as can be witnessed in the Roman hourglass mills and some of the hand querns.[1] In the very early hand querns the cone shape of the bed stone no doubt enabled the slowly revolving concave runner stone to be held in place prior to the development of a satisfactory tentering device for the rotating upper stone.

The cone shaped under runner mill was formerly more numerous in Colonial North America than at first realized. Examples of these mills in the Flory Collection were used for the attrition of various products besides grain as will be seen elsewhere in the text.

A large pair of grain grinding stones were acquired by Mr. Flory following the demise of fellow millstone collector Jacob Brooks. The mill consists of a

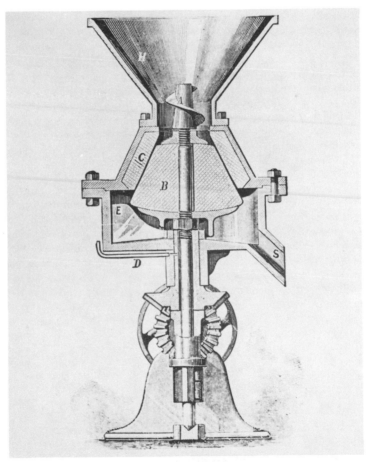

A sectional view of a Ross conical stone mill. The underrunner (B) revolves with a concave, stationary pot lined with dressed segments of stone "C". A scraper "E" discharges the end product through a spout "S". (From Charles Ross and Son Co. Catalog, 1919).

cone under runner and its stationary vase-shaped mate, both hewn out of solid blocks of a conglomerate sandstone, or millstone grit. The heavy stationary stone was mounted on a stout hurst frame with the tapered end facing upwards. The material to be ground was metered into the square top aperture in this stone forming a small hopper and was reduced by the revolving under runner rotating against its smoothed tapered interior surface.

The under runner is deeply socketed on its lower, widest end to allow the fitting of a four-armed fixed rynd on which the stone was mounted and rotated. A vertical three and a quarter inch hole was cut through the center of the stone to accommodate the upper end of the stone spindle which was aligned and wedged firmly to the stone. The upper end of the spindle was attached to a sweep to allow the under runner to be turned by a draft animal walking in a circular path. The lower end bore in a bridging box mounted on a bridge tree allowing the stone to be adjusted in a vertical plane and giving the required gap between the grinding surfaces. The stone had coarse sickle dressing radiating out from around its upper end down to approximately a half of its grinding face. This deep sickle dressing is heavily cracked on the obtuse face of the furrows with no intermediate lands. The lower remainder of that face is left smooth except for continuations of the deep cracking from above.

This type of mill was commonly used for provender (feed) grinding before being ousted on the farm by the hammer mill. It would be particularly suitable for grinding whole dried corn on the cob for livestock feeding as was recorded in the Mid Atlantic and Southern States prior to the innovation of proprietary corn shelling machines in the 1830's.[2]

Several small examples of this type of mill are displayed at the McHargue mill at the Levi Jackson Wilderness Road State Park near London, Kentucky, U.S.A. One pair of stones is assembled in this tiny water mill which is under driven by the shaft of a horizontal water wheel.

Charles Ross and Sons Company, among other mill furnishers in the late 19th Century, advertised a number of mills with conical under runner stones which ran either in vertical or horizontal plane. These mills could be used to grind a wide variety of products ranging from dry grinding of cereal, coffee, drugs, spices, minerals, etc. to material in water, oil, liquid or semi paste form such as paints, ointments, lubricating greases and compounds. They were advertised as being "especially adapted where a large capacity is required with small or limited power and space, and where it is desirous to have the material ground very cool, as the grinding is done on a small circumference running at a high speed so that the material passes through in a moment not remaining long enough to become heated". The text and illustrations from Ross Company Catalogs c. 1920's explain the construction and operation of these mills.

---

[1]Examples of hourglass mills can be seen in the excavated Roman town of Pompeii, Bay of Naples, Italy, and elsewhere. For further text and illustrations of hourglass mills and early queerns see:

Bennett and Elton, "History of Cornmilling", Vol. 1, Chapter VI.
L. A. Moritz, *Grain Mills and Flour in Classical Antiquity,* Chapter XI.
Storck and Teague, *Flour for Man's Bread,* pp. 78-80.
[2]Schlebecker, p. 121.

MIDDLINGS REGRINDING STONES

Middlings, the coarse bits of the floury part of the wheat berry with which small bits of bran may still be associated, are produced in the normal process of grinding wheat to produce fine flour. The middlings are separated together with larger flakes of bran from the fine flours in a bolting machine's fine mesh screens and a purifier.

The "new process" of milling was adopted by many American merchant mills just prior to the introduction of successful roller milling systems to maximize flour extraction and consequently profit. This method used purifiers to extract fine patent flours and the middlings were reground in smaller stones to extract the flour still adhering to the bran. These small stones usually having diameters of two to three feet were often referred to by American millers as "pony stones" to distinguish them from the regular "work horse" millstones that initially ground the wheat. The latter stones were usually made from French burr. In order to successfully extract the "bonus flour" from the middlings, the stones had to be well balanced and level. Critical attention was also given to the shallow dressing of the furrows to keep the stones "sharp". Because much of the tough bran had been removed in the first stage grinding, the miller had to be careful not to put too much pressure on middlings while regrinding or the flour released would be over-heated by friction and "killed". The bread made from it would have poor rising properties. The amount of power required to regrind middlings was recommended to be approximately one tenth of that to grind whole wheat. Because of the risk of choking the eye of the runner stone with the coarse middlings to be reground, it was usual to fix a paddle to the damsel (if the stone was under-driven) or the quant (if over-driven) which ensured a good feed into the stones.

The pair of pony stones in the Flory Collection are quarter dressed with four straight furrows to the harp.

Middlings were accumulated in the normal operation of a merchant mill. They were rejected from the boltings and purifing of several initial grinds and when sufficient quantity was available they would be run through the pony stones. The flour produced on this secondary grind would be again bolted and the resulting flour mixed with the fine and superfine flours bolted off after the initial grind. The remainder that did not make the grade on the second bolting was used for such things as ship's biscuits, and the coarser "brown stuff" or offal would go for animal feed. If the middlings were not reground, the larger particles, known in the trade as semolina, were sometimes used to manufacture such products as macaroni and spaghetti.

A good illustration of the layout of a "New Process Mill" using millstones and purifier, is found in, *"Practical Milling,"* by Prof. B. W. Dedrick, and in the text of *Flour for Man's Bread*, by Storck and Teague, p. 214.

SINGLE ROLLER MILL

The scant remains of this mill, the wooden framework having long since disintergrated, may appear insignificant. However, the prototype of this design of mill, first documented by Bockler in 1662 is the direct ancestor of the modern roller mill which now holds the pre-eminent position in commercial flour milling.[1] Bockler's mill also represents one of the earliest examples of a combined mill and bolter which became so popular after the turn of the present century in the smaller merchant flour mills.[2]

A reconstruction of this type of mill would show the stone roller was rotated by a crank handle on the end of the iron axle secured through the stone's axis; or in later versions, it could no doubt be driven by a small stationary engine with belts and pulleys. The roller is eccentric to the adjacent concave block. Grinding, both shearing and crushing, took place in a straight line in this mill rather than the spiral path all over the surface taken by grain in a regular horizontal millstone. It is easy to see how a second roller could be substituted for the concave block to form the basis of a modern roller mill. This pregnant concept, however, lay dormant for nearly two centuries before being fully appreciated! The meal from the mill fell down into a bolter which was agitated by levers and worked off the same axle that rotated the millstone.

During the transition period from millstones to roller milling in the last quarter of the 19th Century there was much conflict of ideas and interests between the exponents of the two forms of milling. Among the many "patent" mills, millstone dresses, and other devices with exaggerated claims that the exuberant advertising of that period attempted to foist on the market, was the "Bockler Mill." The particular example in the Flory Collection was retrieved from a farm where it had served a useful life in grinding feed. By setting the roller slightly further away from the concave stone, the mill could produce cracked, or rolled oats, wheat, or barley, which came into vogue for animal feed. Later, steel versions of this form of mill were also marketed for this purpose.[3]

---

[1]G. A. Bockler, *Theatrum Machinarum Novum,* published 1662. A collection of plates and descriptions of mechanical devices. Plate 1 depicts this mill.

[2]Example is Midget Marvel Mill perhaps first self contained mill; invented and designed by A. R. Tattersall of London, England, and manufactured in USA by the Anglo American Milling Company of Owensboro, Kentucky.

[3]E. H. Knight, *American Mechanical Dictionary,* Boston, 1876, Vol. 2., p. 1021. In the supplement, is an illustration of a mill with a steel cylinder and steel concave used in Switzerland for cracking wheat. See also, *American Miller,* (Chicago, 1894), Vol. 22., p. 426.

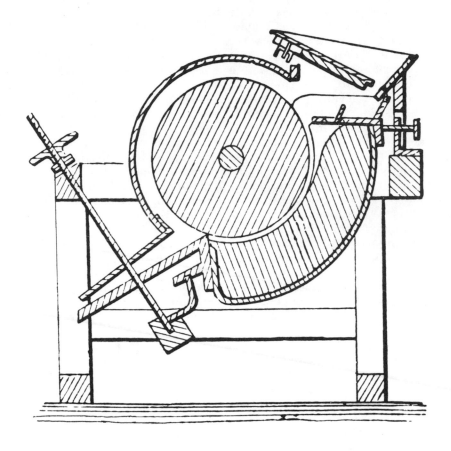

Plan of an improved Bockler type mill. A stone roller revolved adjacent to a stone concave bed. The bed could be aligned by spring loaded adusters. Other versions had adjustable rollers. (Illustration from Knight's, *American Mechanical Dictionary).*

SMALL HIGH SPEED MILLSTONES

Over the centuries there has been a gradual reduction in the diameter of horizontal millstones in mills powered by forces other than human endeavor. Until the late 18th Century it was not uncommon to find millstones in watermills of six or seven feet diameter! These heavy, usually monolithic, stones could be expected to rotate at between 83 and 72 r.p.m. slowly grinding the grain.[1] Most of them had inefficient dress patterns with few quarters of many furrows. Sometimes, there were as many as six furrows per quarter each with a different draft circle. This dress resulted in overheating of the meal and low production relevant to the energy expended in driving the mill.

The Industrial Revolution, accompanied by a rapid population growth, taxed the millwrights ingenuity and skill to increase production. The skilled craftsman of the earlier ages became an engineer. Improved gear profiles, lighter shafting and improved bearings (made possible by increased production of cast and wrought iron) became the order of the day.[2] Millstones became smaller and faster by the second quarter of the 19th Century. The common size of a millstone for a newly erected or refurbished wind or watermill was between forty eight and fifty six inches and was expected to rotate at approximately 100-125 r.p.m.

Experimentation in the late 1840's and 50's with small, high speed "portable" mills accompanied by centrifugal feeding devices slowly overcame prejudices within the milling trade. A report of the 1860's stated that "portable mills with the centrifugal feeding principle can be run (say three foot diameter stones) with an economy of power over large stones of from twenty-five to thirty-three percent and the flour, from its superior liveliness, is preferred by bakers".[3]

During the latter half of the 19th Century, the millstone making industry was transformed from a craft into a science. Assisted by accurate iron casting and machining, mills could be built with a much higher degree of balance and finesse, allowing higher operating speeds and greater and more consistent quality of end product. Just prior to the roller milling revolution, the art of stonedressing had reached a high peak of perfection with much improved and efficient patterns of dress. A number of mill furnishing firms developed fast revolving mills with small diameter millstones which reduced the stress and wear set up by inbalance. They were also economical in the use of expensive, often imported, high quality stone such as the French burr. When using French burr, a single block of stone could be shaped into a millstone having consistency of texture throughout which was extremely difficult to achieve in the large horizontal millstones made of selected keyed blocks. Several manufacturers advertised mills with stones which ran either in a vertical or horizontal plane and could be used to grind a wide variety of products. They afforded a large capacity with minimal power input and space. Because of the high speed and improved dress, the product was reduced without overheating. The better mills had a dress of equal length furrows either of straight or circular form or only one subsidiary furrow to the master in each quarter. In the present century, composite millstones have become increasingly popular because of their even texture and good, consistant, abrasive qualities.

The small portable mills avoided the large capital commitment of the older and larger mills. Many country stores throughout the USA were able to

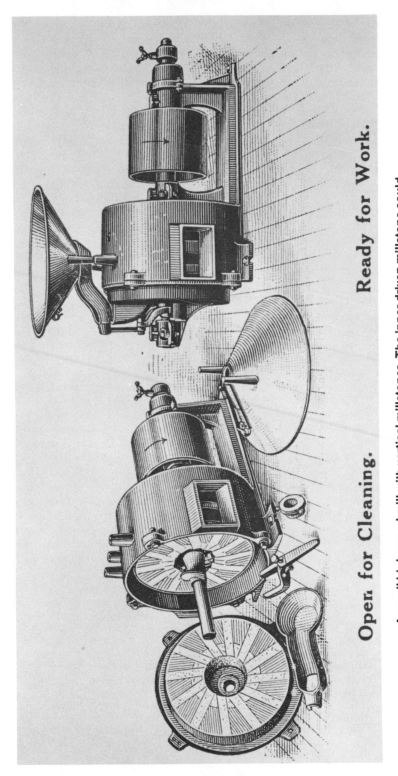

Open for Cleaning.

Ready for Work.

A small high speed mill with vertical millstones. The inner driven millstone could be adjusted with a screw and locknut on the outer end of the horizontal drive shaft. A heavy relief spring prevented damage to the mill caused by accidental ingress of hard or foreign material. (Illustration from Charles Ross and Son Co. Catalog, #20, 1917).

produce cheap flour and meal for local consumption and many farmers invested in this type of mill so avoiding the time-consuming and laborious visits to the local custom mill. These two factors played a major part in the demise of the rural custom mill. Better roads and motorized transport, bringing cheap, standardized products from the huge factory mills, also contributed to the custom mills' demise.

The Flory Collection had a number of examples of stones from these portable mills. Some were retrived from farms in Pennsylvania. Others (used for a wide range of products from industrial grinding to small batches for laboratory testing) came from Charles Ross & Co. Their sizes ranged from eight inches to three feet. There are both flat and conical stones, to run in either a horizontal or vertical plane and in over or under runner mills. The composition of the millstones varied from French burrs and hard American burrs, such as Esopus stone, to composite material such as granulated French burr, Emery, Quartz and Carborundum, etc. Examples of the speed of these mills are quoted from the Ross Company literature for their products.

Type	Diameter of Stone	R.P.M.
Conical Burr Stone Mill	10"	600-1,000
Vertical Stone Dry Mill	16"	400-600
Under Runner Dry Mill	30"	250-400

The speed varied with the application of the mill.

---

[1]Numerous references to old type millstones of between five and seven feet diameter e.g. *Peak Millstones and Hallamshire Grindstones* by Jeffrey Radley, M.A. Excerpt Transaction of the Newcomen Society, Vol. XXXVI, 1963-64; and W. C. Hughes in *The American Miller and Millwrights Assistant* first published 1855. Hughes also states the advantages of reducing the diameter of millstones to approximately four and a half feet and increasing the thickness of the runner stone which considerably reduces the power required to drive them and increases the output of meal from the smaller stones from between twice and five times that expected of the larger older type stones powered by the "old plan of mill building." Page 89-90 revised edition 1884, published Philadelphia.

A standard formula for the velocity of millstones given in a number of early to mid 19th Century millwrights compendium states that their velocity ought to be between 1,550 to 1,600 feet per minute. Therefore divide 500 by the diameter of a millstone in feet or 6,000 by the diameter in inches and the quotient is the number of revolutions required per minute.

[2]See Louis C. Hunter, *Waterpower A History of Industrial Power in the U.S. 1780-1930.* (Published University Press of Virginia, 1979), Chapter 9 particularly, pp. 456-461.

[3]J. Leander Bishop, *A History of American Manufactuers from 1606 to 1860,* Vol. III, (pub. Philadelphia, 1868), page 271. John T. Noye's developed the centrifugal feeding portable mill commencing manufacture in Buffalo, New York, U.S.A. in 1852.

CIDER MILLS

2

A cider pomace mill where apples were crushed under the weight of an edge runner stone. (Illustration from W. H. Pyne, *Picturesque Views of Rural Occupations in Early 19th Century England*).

Cider, the fermented product of apple juice, has long been a favored drink in many European countries. To many North Americans, cider signifies unfermented apple or other fruit juices, and most are unfamiliar with the fermented hard cider popular with our forefathers.

The Romans knew at least thirty six different varieties of apples listed by Pliny the Elder in his *"Natural History"*. Much experimentation and hybridization of improved varieties of apples were carried out in France and England from the medieval period onwards. The British and other Colonials brought their favorites with them to the New World. As early as 1629 apple trees were flourishing in Virginia, and by the early 18th Century cider was the customary drink.

A preliminary stage in the making of cider is the crushing of selected and cleaned apples into pulp or mash known as pomace. An early device used to make pomace was the "stone mill". It consisted of a large circular stone trough in which ran a heavy edge runner. Where timber was plentiful, the runner was often made of wood. They were once relatively common, and barring minor regional variation, conformed to the following basic pattern.

The apples were shoveled into the trough. The edge runner, rotating on a horizontal axle pivoting round a post in the center of the trough, was hauled round by a horse or other draft animal hitched to the axle with a halter and rope. The apples and pulp were pushed into the path of the edge runner by a hand held "stirrer". The animal continued to walk round in a circle until all the apples in the trough were crushed into pulp and the mash resembled a coarse apple sauce and contained skin, core and seeds mixed together, no farmer bothering in those days to core the apples to remove the seeds. A few authorities claimed that the seeds tainted the juice and that perfect cider could not be made with seeds in the pomace. The pomace was then scraped together with a "reever" or pomace rake, then shoveled out of the trough with a wooden shovel and then often allowed to stand to give it a darker color before the juice was extracted using a press.

The example in the Flory Collection is a red sandstone trough in which ran an edge runner. A limestone edge runner from a different mill bears the date 1748 and a heart clearly carved on it. The twelve inch wide working face of this edge runner was flat with no artificial dressing as in the tan bark mill. The shear weight of the revolving stone was sufficient to make pulp of the soft apples.

The stone pomace mill exemplifies the versatility of the "edge runner mill" which has been adapted to reduce materials as varied as rocks to extract minerals to apples and olives to extract juice and oil.

---

[1] Vrest Orton, *The American Cider Book*, (Farrar Straus and Giroux, New York), 1973. See also, Proulx and Nichols, *Sweet and Hard Cider,* (Garden Way Publishing, Charlotte, VT), 1980. Contains good bibliography of cider making.

COCOA AND CHOCOLATE INDUSTRY

The explorer and conquistador, Cortez, introduced into Spain the secret of a new beverage called *"chocolatl"* made by the natives of the New World. The name cocoa is derived from the Aztec word *cacahoatl* which the Spanish contracted to cocao. Eventually the beverage spread to other Western European Countries, and by the middle of the 17th Century chocolate houses were in vogue in England and Germany and the chocolate industry was born. The world's largest chocolate manufacturing plant is located at Hershey, Pennsylvania. A number of stones used to grind cocoa beans were obtained from Hershey for the Flory Collection.

Pods containing approximately 20-40 raw beans are cut from the cacao tree which flourishes only in the tropics and grows best nearest the Equator. When received by the chocolate manufacturer, the dried cacao beans are throughly cleaned to remove any foreign material, roasted for approximately forty minutes in revolving ovens, and then quickly cooled to prevent further change from their own heat. The beans are then passed through rollers which crack the brittle outer shells and break the kernels into smaller pieces called nibs. After the nibs have been cleaned and all the shell removed, the main chocolate making process begins with a prolonged process of grinding and regrinding.

a) The Nib Milling Process:

Formerly, the nibs were ground at Hershey in milling units consisting of three pairs of steel encased granite horizontal millstones one below the other. The granite millstones were gradually superseded by more effective man-made carborundum stones from the late 1930's. The grinding was progressively finer from top to bottom and each pair of stones in a mill were dressed differently for their specific job. Cacao butter, which constitutes about 54% of the bean, was liquified by the frictional heat generated by the grinding and the resulting rich liquor was the basis of all forms of chocolate.

Hershey was operating 87 of these units as recently as 1978 which included 34", 36" and 38" diameter mills. Two units have been retained in the department for "old times sake". The Company dressed their own stones and made major repairs to a stone if it was broken.

Specification drawings of the later stones made by the Carborundum Company of Niagara Falls, New York, depict the varied dress layout for the different pairs of stones. The top pair of a 40" mill had 24" equally spaced straight furrows of three quarters of an inch depth with draft circle of 2½ inches. The lands had circle dress feathers (or cracking) and a 20 inch diameter steel breaker plate fitted in a recess round the eye. The stones of the number two and number three 36" diameter mills had 16 circle dress furrows of 16" radius which gradually decreased in depth from three quarters of an inch to zero in the skirt. The lands were feathered with circle dress of 15" radius. All stones were of left hand dress.

After the nibs had been milled by the above mills the process of making chocolate began. If baking chocolate was being made the next step was more grinding, first by three water cooled steel rollers and then finish grinding in "conches" (or longitudinals), or melanges.

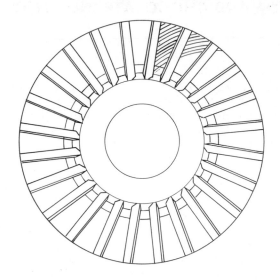

Top Millstone for No. 1 Cocoa Nib Mill

Diameter of Stone 39″
Diameter of Eye 20″
Diameter of Draft Circle 2½″
Furrows 2″ wide x ¾″ deep

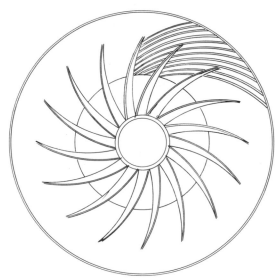

Lower Millstone for No. 2 and No. 3 Cocoa Nib mills (34″ Mill)

Diameter of Stone 33″
Diameter of Eye 6″
Radius of Furrows 14½″
Radius of Cracking Feather 15″
Width of Furrow at Eye 1¼″
Depth of Furrow at Eye ¾″

Three tier nib mills formerly employed by the Hershey Chocolate Co. Cocoa beans were gradually reduced to a butter-like consistency through the three pairs of underrunner millstones. (Photo courtesy of the Hershey Chocolate Co.).

b) Conches and Melangeurs

A melangeur (or Melange - French word for mixture) is a specific type of pan or chaser mill using edge runner stones. A melangeur for making larger batches of chocolate usually comprised of two fixed rollers suspended above and rotated by a revolving pan and the material on the bed of the pan moving under the rollers. The Hershey melangeurs had granite rollers turning against a granite pan bed and these followed the usual practice for the industry. The function of the melangeur was to mix very viscous masses and break up lumps to produce a fine, even-textured, liquor.

The melangeurs with smooth surfaced rollers and beds were later replaced at Hershey with conches, or longitudinals, which comprised of long oblong tubs with corrugated bottoms over which passed corrugated granite rollers. In these heavy duty machines the chocolate liquor was ground and agitated for 96 hours until it had attained the proper degree of fineness and rich mellow flavor. When this had been tempered and poured into moulds to cool, the resulting bars are known as baking chocolate, the kind that is used in every day cooking and the manufacture of some types of chocolate candy.

Information supplied by Hershey Chocolate Company.

A chocolate liquor melangeur. The pan with its granite floor revolves below the stationary granite edge runners, or chasers. Hand wheels on the top frame could raise or lower the chasers to regulate the pressure on the chocolate in the pan. (Illustration from Charles Ross and Son Co. Catalog, 1917).

36

CORK MILL

Cork or "Corkwood" of commerce is the outer bark of an evergreen oak tree *(Quercus suber)* which is native to Portugal, Spain, Southern France and around the Western Mediterranean.

The corkwood is stripped for the first time when the tree is about twenty five years old. This first stripping is known as virgin cork. The coating of outer bark is renewed by nature in about a decade, and from the third stripping forward the average tree yields cork of the quality required for bottle stoppers and other natural cork products every eight to ten years throughout its life of a century or more.

The trees are de-barked in July and August, at which time the dead outer bark is easily pried away from the inner living bark. The strips of cork are then boiled in huge vats which softens it so that it can be flattened for convenient packing. The coarse heavy woody bark is then scraped off and edges trimmed. The cork is afterwards dried, graded, and shipped to cork manufacturers. Most of the annual corkwood production is ground up and used for the manufacture of various cork compositions, including corkboard insulation for refrigerated units, cork pipe covering for cold pipes, gaskets and floor tile.

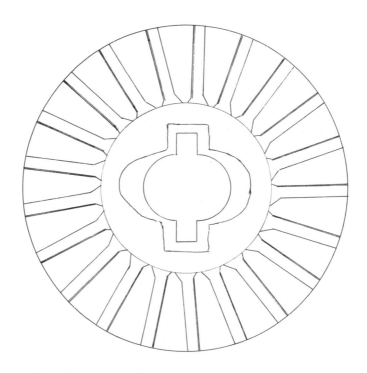

This drawing shows the dress pattern for an Armstrong Cork Co. millstone. The leading edge of the equal length furrows are laid out from the center of the stone's eye thus having no draft circle. (Drawing by the author from the original stone in the Flowerdew Hundred Collection, Hopewell, VA).

Several cork grinding stones were obtained from the Armstrong World Industries Inc. (Formerly Armstrong Cork Co.) Lancaster, Pennsylvania, where cork was ground until 1974.

Baled corkwood received at Armstrong's was carefully graded and its moisture content checked. The reduction process is briefly described as follows: The stored, baled cork was passed into the Breakers Department where a steel rotary action bale breaking machine broke the cork into two inch pieces. It was further reduced and passed through ¾" screens for most purposes. The cleaned broken cork was then conveyed into the mill department.

From the cork mill storage bins, the cork was passed through a steel attrition mill in which the blades could be set to cut the cork to various sizes. The attrition mill plates rotated at a speed of approximately 3,500 r.p.m. The cork was then passed to the stone mills where the final grinding to size was accomplished. The main advantage of a stone mill was that the grinding action would soften and shred the cork. Ground cork from both the attrition and stone mills was passed through a series of centrifugal reel bolters to extract cork of the desired fineness. Cork rejected by the dresser was passed for further grinding in the stone mills. Cork dust is highly inflammable and great precautions were taken at the Lancaster Plant to extract the dust at all points in the mill.

A virtually unused stone of an Armstrong Co. Cork mill. Note the deep bosum, thickness of the stone, and iron hoops around the circumference.

A plan of the mill made in 1943 depicts nineteen pairs of horizontal millstones, each with an upper runner stone and fixed bed stone. The stones were of solid millstone grit from the English Peak District and were found so satisfactory that they were retained until the plant was closed in 1974. A domestic source of stone was sought, but without success. The Flory Collection had one of these substitute stones made from rock of similar texture and color as to English stone, quarried in Indiana County, Pennsylvania. This runner stone was little worn when discarded because the furrows chipped badly at the skirt and its twenty inch thickness gives some indication of the size of the stones when new. Like the English stones, it was hooped with iron to minimize the danger of shattering caused by a fault line in the grit. A bedstone of English millstone grit in the Flory Collection was discarded at the end of its safe working life having been repeatedly dressed down to a thickness of four inches! The deep, right hand, radial dressing occupies only approximately half the radius of the stone the rest being a deeply concave bosom and large eliptical eye partly built up of mortar. The stones ran at a speed of 160 r.p.m., and they were fully exhausted to reduce the risk of combustion of cork dust. The dust was sucked into a wet collector on the roof of the boiler house. Steam was also introduced at the top of each stone mill to reduce fire hazard. The company was very aware of its responsibility towards the health of its employees. It was compulsory that stonedressers wore respirators to prevent silicosis. Many a millstone maker and dry flint mill operator of old would have avoided the agony, lung incapacity, and much reduced life span, if he had been similarly protected from the ravages of this dread disease.

---

[1]*Cork, Its Origin and Many Uses,* (Booklet published by Armstrong Cork Company, Lancaster, Pennsylvania), 1930.

[2]Information on cork mill procedure obtained from correspondence with Armstrong World Industries and Mr. C. E. Sawyer, assistant plant manager at Lancaster, PA.

DYE MILLS

The grinding of vegetable matter to extract dyestuffs has been practiced since ancient times. Vegetable dyes were used to a very considerable extent until late in the 19th Century. As the demand for raw materials increased, plants were cultivated on an increasing scale. For example, indigo was raised extensively in South Carolina in the 18th Century, some of the finest in the world coming from that Colony before its cultivation gave way to the raising of cotton. Indigo was the most important dye employed in colonial manufacturing.[1]

Other sources of dyestuffs were from the leaves of woad and sumac, the petals of sunflower, the roots of madder, the bark of the walnut tree and nutgalls. Alum, copperas, and barilla or soda ash were also used. As can be imagined, a number of different types of mills were employed to crush the varied materials. Edge runners were often used to crush the leaves of indigo, woad and sumac.[2] Special forms of mortar and pestles were often used in the 18th and early 19th Centuries. Gregory described one which consisted of a hard stone or marble mortar in which moved a pear shaped, groved pestle with an iron axis in the upper part. The handle formed part of the axis. The pestle

A hand operated quern for preparing vegetable dyes at a small woollen mill formerly located in Lancaster County, Pennsylvania. (Photo courtesy of the Smithsonian Institution).

was confined in slits in wooden arms so that it could be rotated in a fixed position in the mortar.[3] Another version using two ball mullers rotating in a stone mortar was described and illustrated by Barlow.[4] Logwood mills to crush and grind exotic woods are also described by Barlow; some of these mills used edge runners.[5] Once the dyestuff had been extracted much of it was made up into paste and bars for sale to textile mills.

The carefully fashioned granite hand quern in the Flory Collection came from a small woolen mill in Lancaster Co., Pennsylvania. The runner stone, rotated by a handle socketed into the upper surface, ran within a raised lip carved out of the bed stone. The runner stone was held above the bedstone in the usual way by an iron rynd and spindle and the gap between the stones could be adjusted by inserting a wedge below the stone spindle. The quern could be used either to break up previously prepared bars of dyestuff or to prepare dyestuff from raw materials. The "V" shaped spout formed out of the outer lip of the bedstone suggests that the dyestuff was ground in a paste or liquid form and the resulting dye solution run off into a tub. The dye would then be transferred to a dye bath where hanks of wool, silk, cotton and other textile yarns would be immersed. The quern would have been adequate for making small batches of dyestuff for the small woolen mill. Many small, rural mills developed from the cottage industries of the colonial period in America.

Similar hand quern were also used by potters for preparing batches of glaze materials, and also for grinding color pigments in paint and color wash manufacture.[6]

---

[1]Victor S. Clark, *History of Manufacturers in the United States,* (Published by McGraw-Hill Book Co., New York, 1929), Vol. I, p. 333.

[2]Beauvais-Laseau, *L'art De l'indigotier,* Illustrations of dye Edge Runner Mills.
A History of Technology, Oxford, 1956.
Clark and Wailes, "The Preparation of Woad in England," *Transactions of The Newcomen Society,* Vol. XVI, 1935-36.

[3]G. Gregory, *Dictionary of Arts and Sciences,* (New York, 1821), Vol. 2.

[4]P. Barlow, *Manufacturers and Machinery of Great Britain,* (Published by Baldwin and Cradock, London, 1836), Plate XXXVI.

[5]Logwoodmill preserved at Keynsham Avon, England. Employed edge runner stones. Present plant dates from 1875, last operated in 1964.

[6]John Bivins, Jr., *The Moravian Potters in North Carolina,* (University of North Carolina Press, 1972), p. 81. Examples survive in collections of the Moravian Potters at Old Salem, North Carolina.

FLINT GRINDING MILLS

Two sets of stones from edge runner or "pan mills" were salvaged from former flint mills in York County, Pennsylvania, where, until the late 19th Century, there was a concentration of these mills to supply ground flint for the pottery industry and for cleaning and polishing fine jewelry. The more complete set of stones were from the Bair Mill approximately eleven miles southeast of York which was demolished after the state had acquired the valley where the mill stood for a flood control project in the 1930's.

John Dwight of Fulham, England, is credited with first using "calcined", beaten and sifted flints by 1698.[1] Immigrant master potters from European Countries, including Britain and Germany, introduced flint as a glazing ingredient into the American Colonies by the second quarter of the 18th Century, and throughout much of that century used the finely ground flint for making the white clay dip and other glazes. The bulk of any glaze is made up of silica which occurs in nature as flint or quartz. A common glaze used in the colonies at that time was made from flint, red or white lead, and kaolin.

From the late 18th Century onwards, as transport became less costly and improved flint grinding methods were introduced, flint was increasingly used with pipe clays for the body of the ware imitating popular white and cream wares imported from such established potters as Josiah Wedgewood of Staffordshire, England. Flint whitened the body and reduced the risk of warping. Modern earthenware comprises approximately 32% flint.

Flint nodules gathered from chalk beds were first calcined in a brick lined kiln charged alternatively with flints and coal slacks, or charcoal, in a ratio of approximately twenty tons of flint to one ton of coal.[2] Calcining the flints disrupts the natural crystalline structure and renders them easier to pulverize.

In early days, the calcined flints raked from the cooled kiln were crushed by stamp mills, edge runner stones, and even grist millstones.[3] Fine powdered flint produced by these dry grinding methods produced a lethal atmosphere for the operatives; incapacity and premature death from silicosis, or "potters rot" as it was known in the English potteries, was rampant.

Increasing demand for ground flint, and the high mortality rate among flint mill workers, led to the introduction of wet grinding processes. The wet grinding of flint by edge runners was patented in Britain by Thomas Benson in 1726 with modifications in 1732 which included the use of stone in place of iron rollers which tended to contaminate the end product.[4]

The stone mills in the Flory Collection are representative of a two stage reduction of flint to powder. The edge runners and base are all hewn out of solid granite quarried from the cliffs overlooking Port Deposit on the Susquehanna River near the Maryland-Pennsylvania State line, a few miles west of Interstate 95. The circular base or trough is 72" diameter with a smooth track carved on the outer lip on which trundled two bell-shaped edge runners. Their grinding faces, rounded to form the required angle of nip to contain and crush the flint, fit the contour of the trough in the base.[5] The calcined and wetted flints were shoveled into the concave trough and gradually crushed by the rollers each weighing approximately 3,800 lbs. into the consistency of sand.

The runners revolved round a stout, vertical, pivot post secured at its lower end in a square socket in the round, raised, center boss. Four anchor bolts retained a collar round the pivot post. Each of the runners which were geared together had eleven inch square holes cut through their axis points to facilitate the horizontal axles. The usual speed of these older sets of smooth rolls was about 15-25 r.p.m.[6]

A flint grinding millstone from York County, Pennsylvania. Calcined flint was initially crushed beneath the two large edge runners in the granite pan and finally reduced to fine powder in a secondary mill employing the small roll in the background. (Photo courtesy of the Smithsonian Institution).

The flint from this first reduction was transfered to a second pan mill where smaller rollers weighing about 400 lbs. reduced the flint to a slurry. The slurry was then heated in ovens to drive off the water by evaporation and then passed through fine sieves to achieve the desired end product.

A variation in the method of achieving the second and final reduction of flint, once common in the English Potteries, and elsewhere, consisted of a pan mill where the flint slurry was ground between a stone base, usually made up of blocks of silica rich chert, and large blocks of chert pushed around inside the pan by paddles.[7]

The grinding of flint by the edge runner and pan mill method was rendered obsolete by steel ball mills or cylinder grinding mills. At present, the continuous grinding in Hardinge mills and vibro energy separators are the norm.[8]

---

[1]A. R. Mountfor, *Illustrated Guide to Staffordshire Salt Glazed Stoneware,* (London, 1971), p. 36. Also, M. Birnson, *John Dwight, Transactions of English Ceramic Circle,* 1961, Vol. 5, part 2, pp. 95-109.

[2]Robert Copeland, *A Short History of Pottery, Raw Materials and the Cheddleton Flint Mill,* (Cheddleton Flint Mill Industrial Heritage Trust, Hanley Stoke on Trent, England, 1972), p. 15.

[3]John Bivins, Jr., *The Moravian Potters in North Carolina,* (University Press, 1972), p. 18. Quote: - *"This afternoon the mill was run for the first time; the saw mill is not yet ready, and the dam is not finished. The mill was first tried in grinding flint for glazing, it made a fine powder. Then it was a difficult task to remove the upper millstone, clean it and recut it. Then a little corn was ground, and finally two bushels of wheat . . . it made very nice flour."*

[4]Copeland, p. 6.

[5]Size of the largest pieces that will pass under the runner depends on the angle of nip which differs for different materials according to the following relationship.

$$d = D \tan^2 \theta/2$$

where d = diameter of the largest piece that will pass under the runner, D = diameter of runner, θ = angle of nip.

Generally the harder the material to be crushed the smaller the angle of nip. Thus, if the diameter of the runner is 60", and the angle of nip is 20°, then the largest piece that will pass under the runner will be 1.86". But if a softer material having an angle of nip of 40° is to be ground, the largest piece that will pass under a 60" diameter runner will be about 8".

[6]*Grinding and Crushing - A Bibliography,* (H. M. Stationary Office London, 1958), p. 50.

[7]Copeland.

[8]*Ibid,* p. 17. (See Glossary for definition of terms.)

HEMP MILLS

The tall annual herb *Cannabis sativa,* commonly known as hemp, is a native of Asia. It had long been cultivated and processed in the Old World, and the seeds and technology were brought to North America by the early European colonists.[1] Hemp processing soon became firmly established as a "homespun" industry providing many basic essentials for the fledgling nation.[2] The separated and softened fibers extracted from the stem provided excellent raw material for making cordage, weaving into coarse cloth (including sailcloth, workclothes, and sacking) and also oakum for caulking wooden boats, paper and sundry other products.

Only the outer layers of the hemp stems are utilized and a number of processes have to be undertaken to produce soft, pliable fibers suitable for weaving. These stages are similar in many respects to those used to prepare flax fibers.

Traditionally, the closely planted hemp was uprooted by hand when the male and female plants were fully ripe and tied into small sheaves called baits. If the seed was to be saved for resowing or crushing to extract the oil then the seed pods were cut off, dried and threshed. "Retting" was the first stage in which the baits were sometimes immersed in cool water for one or two weeks. This was called water retting. In North America, the usual practice was to spread out the baits on grass where they were "dew retted" for a period of three to eight weeks.[3] Retting permits bacteria to break down the woody tissues by fermentation, and to dissolve, by enzyme action, the substances binding the fiber cells. After retting the stems were rinsed and allowed to dry before being broken.

Until well into the 19th Century, quantities of hemp and flax for household use were processed by hand tools. Crushing of the stems was accomplished first with a wooden hemp brake, larger but similar in design to a common flax brake. This was carried out preferably in the open air because of the large amount of dust created which is a strong lung irritant. The friable woody portions of the stems were mostly removed by "braking", interspersed with frequent shaking out.

Further cleaning and softening of the fibers was achieved by "scutching" (sometimes called "swingling" or beetling) where the hemp was laid on a vertical board and struck repeatedly with a wooden scutching knife called a "beetle." When the experienced worker considered the fibers were sufficiently clean and pliable, handfulls of hemp were drawn through "heckles" (hatchel or hackles) consisting of closely spaced iron spikes mounted in a wooden base. This process separated the shorter fibers, called tow, from the longer fibers. Tow combed through coarser heckles was used to manufacture cordage and sacks. Fiber from finer heckles was spun into yarn for weaving workcloth and sailcloth.

Specialized stone roller mills were sometimes employed by German and Moravian immigrants to scutch fiber prior to combing through heckles. The stone roller was in the shape of a frustum of a cone. The rollers in the Flory Collection were typical of others to be seen in museums in Pennsylvania and Germany.[4] A tapered hole was bored through the axis to take an iron axle. This axle was fixed to a vertical upright shaft passing through the center of the circular bed of the mill. The roller turned on a hardwood bearing plugged into a recess in the stone around the axle extremity. An arm secured to the vertical

45

shaft above the stone and approximately 45° ahead of the iron axle was attached with a chain to the outer end of the roller's axle. This hauled the roller around in a fixed plane as the vertical shaft was turned by the waterwheel's transmission below. Previously broken and scutched hemp was laid out on the oak floor in the path of the roller and further crushed and softened. The hemp was turned and shaken from time to time and retained in the bed of the mill by the circular iron, or wood, curb. This type of mill traces its ancestry back to Germany.[5] Similar European mills reportedly could soften approximately 90 Kg. of hemp in eight hours.[6]

Stone hemp mills were built in Pennsylvania and nearby states during the later 18th Century and early 19th Centuries. There were approximately twenty hemp mills recorded in Lancaster County, Pennsylvania, by 1810.[7] These mills often ran in conjunction with a saw or grain mill and did custom work. Sometimes a farmer would bring his hemp to the mill, roll it himself and pay for the use of the mill.[8]

Another type of mill once used for preparing hemp fiber was a stamp mill usually having flat, or round nosed wooded stamps, falling into previously scutched hemp held over a wood or stone mortar.[9]

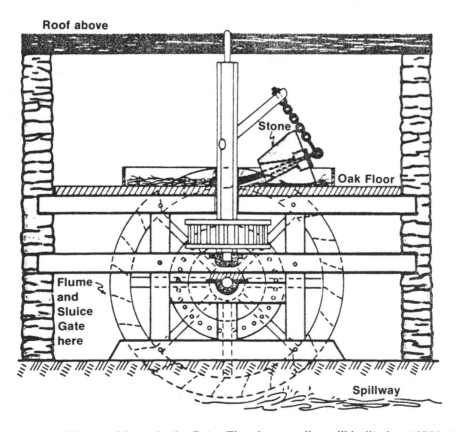

Diagram of the machinery in the Peter Elser hemp roller mill built about 1760 at Clay, Pennsylvania. (Courtesy of Dr. Carter Litchfield).

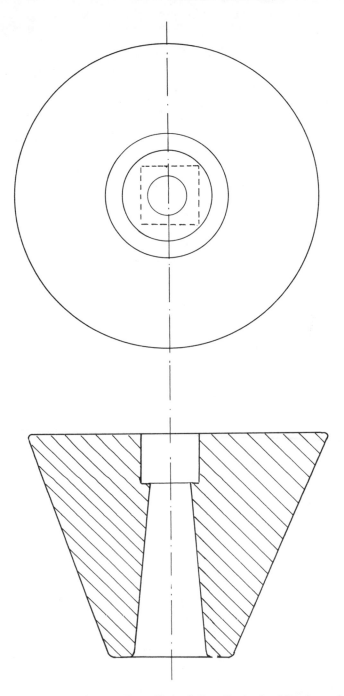

Section through a hemp roller mill depicting the typical frustum of a cone shape. (Drawing by the author after a stone in the Flowerdew Hundred Collection, Hopewell, VA).

Information gathered on the former Pennsylvania and German hemp mills suggest that the roller and stamp mills were used only to soften previously broken and scutched hemp.[10] Some 18th and early 19th Century sources, however, state that these hemp mills were also employed to "brake" the hemp stems.[11] This is contrary to the better practice of the times where the braking process, as stated earlier, should be conducted out of doors, or in well ventilated conditions, to allow the dispersal of lung damaging dust.

The rollers in the Flory Collection, and others seen in Pennsylvania museums, all had smooth working faces although some sources state that fluted rollers were an improvement over smooth rollers.[12] Two sources record hemp mills with rollers running over a corrugated bed of close laid logs which would presumably have a similar action on the help as fluted roller.[13] Later patent hemp brakes are found with a series of cast iron fluted rollers.[14]

Most of these primitive roller mills appear to have become defunct by the mid 19th century. By the 1830's, factory production of textiles in the U.S.A. had virtually taken over from homespun. Cotton had become a staple crop and with it came improved processing machinery. Cotton was "King" in the field of clothing and also ousted flax and hemp for sailcloth in the U.S.A. By the 1850's Kentucky was the chief producer of hemp. Most of its production was for cordage and bagging.[15] Hemp for cordage was gradually eclipsed by manila and jute and later wire ropes became popular for heavy duty work.

------

[1]*Encyclopedia Britannica.* Hemp cultivation was recorded in China as early as 2800 B.C. The ancient Egyptians and other Eastern Mediterranean civilizations processed hemp, and its use spread throughout Europe during the Middle Ages. New World cultivation began with planting in Chile in the 1500's, and in the British North American colonies in the second quarter of the 17th Century.

[2]*Reports from the Navy Department . . . on Water Rotted Hemp,* Doc. 68, House of Representatives, 20th Congress, (Washington, 1828), pp. 4, 8, 27, 30, 32, 33.

[3]Abraham Rees, *Cyclopaedia of Arts, Sciences and Literature,* Vol. XVII (London, 1819), Under the heading "Hemp". Quotes full description of hemp, cultivation and processing.

[4]Collections where hemp mill rollers are on view; Pennsylvania Farm Museum, Lancaster; Mercer Museum, Doylestone; Hans Her House, Willow Street; Colonial Valley, Menges Mill - all in Pennsylvania; Flowerdew Hundred, Virginia. A complete hemp roller mill is on display at the Vogtsbauernhof Open Air Museum, Gutach, Schwartzwald, West Germany.

[5]Friedrich W. Weber, *Die Geschichte der Pfalzischen Muhlen Besonderer Art,* (Otterbach, West Germany, 1981), pp. 215-229.

[6]A. Butowski, *The Means of Improving the Management, Cultivation and Fabrication of Hemp,* (St. Petersburg, Russia, 1842). [English translation by P. Von Schmidt in *The New American State Papers, Agriculture,* Vol. 2, (Wilmington, 1973), pp. 462-464.]

[7]*The Conestoga Expedition of 1902,* reported that Lancaster County had four hemp mills in 1750, about thirteen in 1780, and twenty in 1810. These mills were for preparing hemp and not for spinning or weaving. Mr. Rupp in his *History of Lancaster County* p. 189, published in 1844, stated that Hempfield Township was so called from the great quantities of hemp grown there.

[8]Quoted by Mr. Elser, grandson of Peter Elser builder and proprietor of Clay Hemp Mill, Pennsylvania, in article "Hemp and the Early Hemp Mills of Lancaster County", *The Sunday News,* (Lancaster, Pennsylvania, U.S.A., September 2, 1928), p. 14.

[9]Dr. Carter Litchfield, *Early Pennsylvania Hemp Mills,* transactions of the International Molinological Society, Vol. 5. (in press).

[10]Personal Correspondence with Dr. Carter Litchfield, Newark, Delaware, U.S.A.

[11]Abraham Rees, *Cyclopeadia,* (Chambers Cyclopaedia), Vol. XVII.

[12]*Ibid.*

[13]William S. Webb, "Old Millstones of Kentucky", *The Filson Club History Quarterly,* Vol. 9. No. 4, (Louisville, Kentucky, October, 1935), p. 218. "A somewhat similar method was devised for the breaking of hemp. A stone was cut in the form of the frustum of a circular cone. This stone was designed to be rolled by horse power over a sloping 'corduroy' platform made of small logs and raised some two feet above the earth. The slope of the platform was adjusted to the slope of the stone. A trench, some three or four feet deep, was dug around the edge of the platform, allowing the men to stand upright as they placed the hemp on the platform. The heavy stone rolling over the hemp crushed the stalks and made it possible for the men to shake out the lint from the hurds." A similar account is rendered by J. H. Stoner in an unpublished account of Pennsylvania mills and millstones, particularly relating to Franklin County, PA.

[14]Knight, *American Dictionary of Arts and Sciences",* p. 880.

[15]Victor S. Clark, *History of Manufacturers in United States, 1607-1860,* Vol 1, (McGraw-Hill Book Co., Inc., New York, 1929), pp. 529-533.

PAINT AND COLOR MILLS

As with dyestuffs, paints and color pigments have been used by man since the dawn of history. Primitive mills such as the slab and muller, mortar and pestle, and hand querns, were still being used in America and Western Europe until well into the 19th Century.[1] A number of traditional pigments such as common orpiment, or Kings Yellow, and verdigris are strong poisons. Other such as white and red lead, chrome yellow, and vermilion, are extremely deleterious. The dangerous disease *colica pictonum* cause by white lead poisoning and leading to paralysis and premature aging and lingering death has long been known. Because of these dangers, enclosed mills have been used for many years to reduce these hazards. By the 19th Century, increasingly sophisticated mills were being developed to triturate these substances.[2]

The Flory Collection contained a number of stones pertaining to the industry from mills built by the Ross Company of Brooklyn, New York. This company's range of color and paint mills was typical of others being manufactured in Western Europe and North America from the later 19th Century through the early 20th Century. There were pan or chaser mills, horizontal millstone mills (both underrunners and over runners), vertical stone mills, conical stones, tandem mills, and double eccentric tub mills.

Heavy crushing of materials in a dry or semi-dry state, such as with enamels, was often accomplished in a revolving bed chaser or pan mill. The pan or bedstone revolves carrying the material under the stone rollers which revolve on a fixed horizontal shaft by contact with the bed stone or material on the bed stone. Ross Company also recommended this type of mill for crushing glass, fire clay, and other materials that must be kept free from iron or other metals.

Under or overdriven rollers (or chasers) in a fixed pan were offered for mixing whiting, putty, white lead, mortar colors, roof cements, and other pasty materials. A galvanized sheet steel hood could be fitted on top of the pan to enclose the mill to prevent the escape of toxic dust when dry materials were being crushed or powdered. The mills came in a variety of sizes and could have one or two chasers. Whiting chasers, having a single or pair of stone rollers revolving around a horizontal axle secured and turned by a gear driven vertical mast, ran in a large pan for wet grinding and for floating whiting on a stone base.

A whole range of horizontal stone mills with flat or conical stones, most being equiped with under-runners, were also manufactured. Both Ross and Kent Machine Works Inc., also in Brooklyn,[3] supplied these mills with a choice of Esopus stone, French burr or "hard" American burrs for preparing Japan, coach colors and enamels. The sizes of stones ranged from 8" diameter in a small water-cooled flat stone laboratory mill, to 36" diameter stones recommended for grinding heavy paste paints, lead and color milling, liquid paints, new inks, and also for grinding dry materials, dry colors, etc.

A revolving bed chaser or pan mill used for heavy crushing of material in a dry, or semi-dry state. Enamels, white lead, and fire clay were ground in mills such as this. (From Charles Ross and Son Catalog #9B, 1919).

An under runner mill for preparing Japan, coach color, and enamels. This view shows the hinged top stone raised and hopper thrown back for easy cleaning. Note the improved millstone dress of equal length furrows. (Illustration from Kent Machine Works Inc., Brooklyn, NY, Bulletin "M". No date, circa 1920.)

A double eccentric tub or enamel mill for extremely fine grinding of materials in water. (From Charles Ross and Sons Catalog, 1917)

Tandem mills were also produced with small horizontal stones for double grinding of fine colors in oil, varnish or Japan, and colored leather coatings. The upper millstones were fed from a steel combined mixer, or feeder pot, with an agitator. The material from the upper stones fed from a spout into the eye of the lower pair. Gangs of two to eight tandem mills could be supplied. Each mill had its own clutch so it could be run independently or in line with the others.

Ross made several sizes of conical stone mills with under-runners specially designed for "grinding in oils, varnish, water and other materials in a liquid or semi-paste form. Ross Company literature states that these conical under runner mills were extensively used for ready mixed and liquid paints, lubricating greases and compounds, paste blacking, ointments, meerschaum pulp, cocoa beans and a great variety of articles". The grinding surfaces were of French burr or "American burr" ground in perfectly, and accurately finished, forming a water joint before dressing or cutting in the furrows.

A variation on an old established type of color mill — the flat muller pushed round on a bedstone, as used in the flint mills — was also made by Ross. This was their double eccentric tub or enamel mill. They were built singly or in pairs for grinding in water such materials as enamels, drop blacks, graphite for lead pencils and electrotypes, polishing rouge, ultramarine blue, mica, etc.

Two mills worked on the "molar principle". The material passed down through the center of the runner so that the material was constantly flowing back and reground over and over. The molar or top stone revolved around on the bed stone and was also revolved around on its own axis which gives it a double eccentric motion. The periphery of the runner stone forms perfect epicycloidal curves, so that no two parts of the faces of the stones wear together as they are constantly changing thus wearing both bed and runner stones nearly level. The running of these mills was very simple with no dressing required to the stones and little power required. The charge was drawn out of the tub when it was reduced as fine as desired. Ross built these mills with 20, 30, 36, 42 and 54 inch bed stones.

Other mills for dry grinding such things as enamels and feldspar, for enamelers and pottery, were called drag mills. These are similar to those described in the flint mill section where blocks of chert were dragged round above a similar stone bed in an enclosed pan.

The range of different forms of mills found in the paint and color industry typifies the diversity and versatility of different mills developed over many centuries of trial and error.

---

[1]See illustrations Plate XXXV and text on these mills under heading of "Mechanics" in *Rees Cyclopeadia*.

[2]See text and illustration in Knights, *American Dictionary of Arts and Sciences,* p. 1598; also, *Appletons Dictionary of Machines, Mechanics and Engine Work and Engineering,* Vol. II, (1852), p. 427.

[3]Kent Machine Works Inc., 39 Cold Street, Brooklyn, New York, Founded 1890.

PHOSPHATE ROCK GRINDERS

Three chemical elements, phosphorus, nitrogen and potassium are essential nutrients of both plants and animals. These elements form the major constituents of modern fertilizers required to replace these trace elements in the soil greatly depleted by the increasing intensity and demands of agriculture.

The main source of phosphate in fertilizers is phosphate rock of marine origin. A smaller amount comes from rock of an igneous origin. At one time guano (seabird manure) and rock derived from it were significant sources, but supplies are now virtually exhausted. The commercial quality of phosphate rock is determined by its content of tricalcium phosphate ($Ca_3P_2O_8$) which is known as bone phosphate of lime (B.P.L.)[1].

Specially constructed millstones were used until well into the present century to finish grind the rock. Although a substantial amount of finely ground phosphate rock is applied directly to the soil, the majority is decomposed with acid (usually sulphuric), to make superphosphates or phosphoric acid. These products form the raw materials for many subsequent products in industry.

The special stones in the Flory Collection came from two sources, but are of similar construction. One pair came from the former Lancaster Chemical Company, Lancaster, Pennsylvania. Other used stones, in excellent condition, came from the Ross Company, Brooklyn, New York. Each millstone has a wide, concave, granite bosum. The bosum rocks of the Lancaster millstones are ten sided where they join the outer granulating face. The Ross examples have octagonal sided bosums. The face proper (comprising only the skirt of the millstone) is made up of shaped pieces of blue-gray carborundum (aluminum oxide - Al_2O_3) and Magnetite (iron oxide - Fe_3O_4). Lengths of gray-green rock of like hardness and finely grained texture are cut to the dimensions of the equal length furrows of the left hand straight dress. The wide lands are deeply cracked or stitched with a circle dress, but this does not extend into the bosum as do the furrows. The deep bosum allows the feed easy access and gradually reduces the coarse lumps of phosphate rock before being finally ground to finish size by the granulating face of the skirt.

The construction of these composite stones are interesting in that the pieces of stone are "cemented" together with a lead alloy. Iron balance weights are built into the circumference and iron hoops are shrunk on to give extra strength. The stones appear to have been encased in metal jackets.

A number of millstone manufacturers on both sides of the Atlantic constructed heavy duty stone mills often with French burrs of very hard quality having extra thickness and strongly hooped for grinding cement, lime, phosphate rock, coprolites, barytes and other hard minerals.[3]

---

[1]Arch Fredric Blakey, *The Florida Phosphate Industry,* (Harvard University Press, Cambridge, Massachusetts 1973), p. 9.

[2]*Ibid.*

[3]Reference from trade catalogues published by firms including Chas. Ross & Son Company, New York, and Wm. Garner & Sons, 72 Mark Lane, London, England. (Both catalogues of 1920's.)

A phosphate rock grinder depicting the solid granite bosum and composite skirt of carborundum. (Photo by the author of stone in the Flowerdew Hundred Collection, Hopewell, VA).

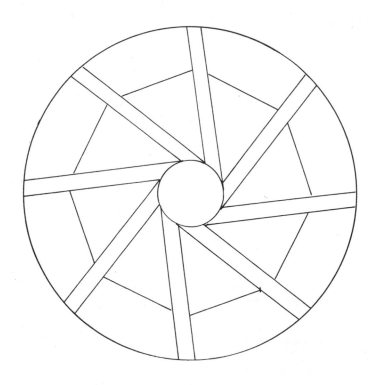

PLASTER OF PARIS AND GYPSUM GRINDING MILLS

Gypsum, or hydrous calcium sulphate, is the most common sulphate mineral occuring in many localities in a variety of forms. When heated or calcined in a kiln to expel its water content, a fine whitish powder can be produced known as plaster of Paris. It is so-called because of the wide fame and long usage of this plaster produced from gypsum quarried from the extensive beds around Montmartre, Paris, France. When water is added to this anhydrous powder it swells, and rapidly sets. It is much used for making molds, casts, wall rendering and a type of cement. It was used to cement together the shaped blocks of burrs in French burr millstones, and holds together the backing balast. It also gives a smooth clean finish to a non grinding face. This greatly eased the balancing of the millstone often assisted with lead or patent balance boxes let into the plaster face. It was also frequently used to this effect in finishing and balancing solid, hand-hewn millstones.

Ground gypsum enjoyed moderate success until the early 19th Century as a fertilizer and stimulant for crops, particularly when used on sandy and gravelly soils. This use was first practiced by Herr Mayer, a German clergyman and farmer about 1768, and had been introduced into North America by the last quarter of the 18th Century. It was popularized in the American Colonies by such advocates at Richard Peters,[1] President of the Philadelphia Society for promoting agriculture, and John A. Binns, who contended that "gypsum, clover, and deep ploughing" were the backbone of his farming success in Loudoun County, Virginia.[2]

An example of stones used for grinding Gypsum with the fixed upper stone on the left, and the frustum of a cone shaped under runner on the right. (Photo courtesy of the Smithsonian Institution).

French and Nova Scotia gypsum was originally used in North America but quarries on Cayuga Lake and other deposits in Western New York State also supplied large tonnages.[3] Gypsum was inexpensive and usually applied in early spring or late autumn at a rate of approximately two bushels an acre.[4]

In Colonial America, gypsum used as land plaster was ground originally by regular millstones and there were a number of references, to the effects, detrimental or otherwise, to these millstones.[5] Numerous local custom mills ground gypsum. The nominal toll for rendering this service in Virginia in the late 18th Century was one eighth of that ground.[6] There are references to mortar and pestle stamping mills and sledge hammers being used for producing land plaster. In 1796, Oliver Evans, the noted American millwright, patented an iron screw mill to break up the larger lumps of gypsum which were then passed through a sieve before being ground into powder by a pair of millstones. Powered by his own steam engine, he had perfected it by 1804 to be able to produce twelve tons in twenty-four hours. Evans sold gypsum as a fertilizer and plaster for stucco work and also in building up French Burr millstones at his works in Philadelphia.[7]

There are several examples in the Flory Collection of the various forms of stone mills that formerly ground gypsum. The most impressive is similar in some respects to that already described in the section on "The under-runner cone type stone". These stones were hewn from a pebble conglomerate. The frustum cone under runner received the broken lumps of gypsum on its coarse spiral shaped furrows and fed it down, grinding them finer and finer on its smoother and radially dressed lower half. The fixed cover stone was dressed similarly. Its operation and mounting are similar to that already described in the "under runner cone stone". Each stone has holes bored in their lower circumferences for the bail pins of a stone crane to facilitate ease of lifting to clean and redress.

---

[1]Peters was a judge in District Court of Pennsylvania and owner of Belmont Estate in Fairmont Park. In 1797, he published a pamphlet giving his results of experiments with land plaster entitled *Agricultural Enquires on Plaster of Paris,* (Fletcher Stevenson Whitcomb, Pennsylvania Agriculture and Country Life, 1640-1840 pub. Harrisburg, 1950).

[2]Binns wrote, *Treatise on Practical Farming,* published in 1803. Further references in *Thomas Jefferson's Farm Book,* edited by Edwin M. Betts, (University Press of Virginia, 1976), p. 195.

[3]Harry B. Weiss and Grace M. Ziegler, *Forgotten Mills of Early New Jersey,* (New Jersey Agricultural Society, Trenton, NJ, 1960), p. 25.

[4]*Ibid.,* p. 25, and *Rees Enclopeadia,* 1818.

[5]*Thomas Jefferson's Farm Book,* pp. 199-200.

[6]*Ibid.,* p. 196.

[7]Bathe, Greville and Dorothy, *Oliver Evans, A Chronicle of Early American Engineering,* (Historical Society of Pennsylvania, 1935). Also, Eugene S. Ferguson, *Oliver Evans,* (Hagley Museum, 1980), pp. 33-34.

TANBARK MILLS

The crushed, dried bark from trees, leaves and plant galls has been used since early civilizations in the process of tanning leather.[1] Until well into the 19th Century, much of the best leather was tanned in a liquor made from crushed bark, preferably oak, and water.

Tannin, containing tannic acid used for tanning, is yielded primarily by the oak, hemlock, chestnut and mangrove. In America, sumac leaves were also a prime source. Scraped and selected skins and hides were laid in a pit containing thick, beer-like, sickly sweet, liquor for up to a month slowly absorbing the astringent tannin which transformed certain proteins of animal tissue into compounds that resist decomposition and turn a perishable hide into fine leather. Oak bark tanning is rarely practiced today as it is considered too slow and costly a process in the world of mass production. The leather so produced is still considered supreme.[2]

Bark was normally peeled from the selected trees using a spud or peeling iron in the spring when the bark peeled easily and contained the maximum quantity of tannin. The removed bark was cut into longitudinal strips and allowed to air dry in storage racks before being corded and sold to a tannery. In Colonial America, the gathering of tanning bark was a sideline of lumbering and clearing of land for farming.

A tanbark crushing mill having one or two edge runners could crush approximately ½ cord of tanbark a day. The runners usually had a deeply corrugated working face. (Picture from, W. H. Pyne, *Picturesque Views of Rural Occupations in Early 19th Century England*).

The 45" diameter edge runner stone of the Flory Collection, with its heavily corrugated 13" wide crushing edge, followed the usual pattern of this type of bark mill. Some bark mills had two edge runners, one of stone and one of wood chasing round in a circular trough hewn from solid stone or made up of slabs. The mills were often powered by draft animals or water power - abundant water supply being a prerequisite for a tannery site.

A tanyard usually employed its own mill to grind the tanbark. It was not ground to a fine powder because the water would act upon it too quickly, also fine powder had a tendency to form an insoluable mass if it became damp. The liquor for tanning was obtained by pouring cold water on the ground bark and leaving it to stand for a few days, it was then passed from one leaching pit to another until the desired strength was achieved.

Morfit stated that in 19th Century Britain, bark was also ground between two horizontal millstones usually having a special form of dressing.[3]

From the end of 18th Century onwards iron superseded stonemills. In 1797, Weldon's bark mill was patented. It consisted of a conical iron drum with teeth that rotated in a toothed iron casing all held in an iron frame. The bark was rasped as it passed between the teeth of the drum and casing.[4] In 1811, another cast iron mill was reputed to grind three times the quantity that could be achieved by a stone mill.[5]

Chrome tanning, the process most common today, based on the use of chrome salts and requiring only a few hours was known as early as 1856, and first patented in the U.S.A. in 1884 by August Schultz.

---

[1]*New Columbian Encyclopedia,* (Columbia University Press, New York and London, 1975), p. 2691. Its use is depicted in Egyptian tomb paintings dating from 3,000 B.C.

[2]Tim Severin, *The Brendan Voyage,* (McGraw Hill Book Company, 1978), Chapter 2. For details of the traditional tanning of ox hides for the leather boat that re-inacted the fabled crossing of the Atlantic by Irish monks in the 6th Century A.D.

[3]Cambell Morfit, *The Arts of Tanning, Currying and Leather-Dressing,* English translation by J. De Fontenelle and F. Malpeyre, (Philadelphia, 1852), Chapter 10. See description of Bagnall's Machine for chopping bark and fleshing hides. Uses horizontal stones. pp. 114-119.

[4]*Ibid.,* pp. 119-122.

[5]Harry B. Weiss, *History of Tanning in New Jersey,* (New Jersey Agricultural Society, Trenton, NJ), p. 30.

A FEW WORDS ON MILLSTONE DRESS

Stone dressing is the preparation of the working face of a millstone to best undertake the purpose it is intended. The dressing style will vary depending on the manufacture of differing end products. Examples include cutting and shearing as in the reduction of wheat for flour; or crushing and grinding as in the reduction of minerals, and in paint manufacture; or rubbing as in the case of a hulling stone.

There are a number of elements involved in the dress layout. The direction of millstone rotation, of course, is dictated by the transmission layout of a mill, and this will decide the direction the furrows will lay. The millstone face is divided into a number of areas. These are the eye, bosum and grinding face proper. The latter is normally divided into lands and furrows. The furrows will vary in duty, number, outline, depth, direction, length, draft, width section and surface.

The eye, through which the material to be processed is fed into the mill, is an element of the dress because it offsets or modifies the action of the furrows. The larger the eye and greater its taper downwards and outwards the easier the feed and less bosum and draft is necessary. There are certain qualifications however to this rule. A number of later small high speed mills had eyes with bevels graduated into the furrows to enhance the feeding qualities.

The bosum allows for easy access of feed and causes the material to be gradually reduced before being finished off on the granulating surface of the true grinding face. The grain miller of earlier centuries using large diameter millstones made much use of the dished bosum. But better practice of the 19th Century called for a wide, very shallow, perfectly even bosum with furrows extending to the eye. In certain applications, such as grinding cork or minerals, a deeper bosum was retained to advantage.

The true granulating face may comprise virtually all the area of the millstone's surface from eye to skirt, or merely a strip next to the skirt. It may be furrowed or not. The subject of which pattern of dress was best for a particular application has been the cause of much heated discussion and conjecture for centuries by those using millstones. For centuries, tradition seemed to dictate the pattern of dress, while the lessons learned through a certain amount of local experimentation were restricted by lack of adequate communication. Some idea of the diversity of thought on the subject can be assessed by the sixty one different patents taken out in the U.S. alone in the period 1830-1873 for grain milling; the majority in the last twenty years of that period.[1]

It is generally agreed that the furrows perform the duties of assisting granulation, cooling, distribution of the "chop" between the faces and carrying it out to the skirt. There are certain reservations to these principals. Stones of suitable texture have been run without furrows and the granulation and distribution was not overly diminished, although the end product was unduly warm. Tests carried out with the furrows reversed did not greatly affect the output of the stones; of course, there is no disputing that a balanced pair of millstone with an approved pattern of dress and running in the correct direction produces a superior product.

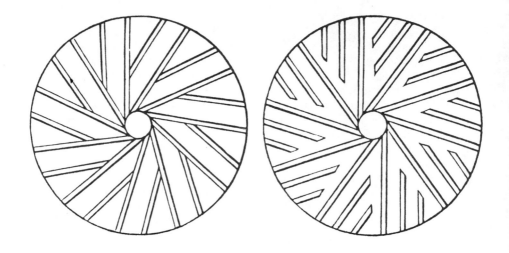

These illustrations depict the main types of millstone dress: "quarter" dress (above), and circular furrow or "sickle" dress (below). The drawings are from *The American Miller and Millwrights' Assistant,* by William Carter Hughes (Detroit, 1850).

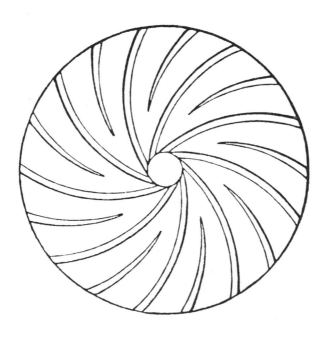

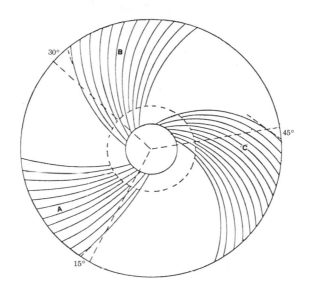

Logrithmic Dress Pattern.

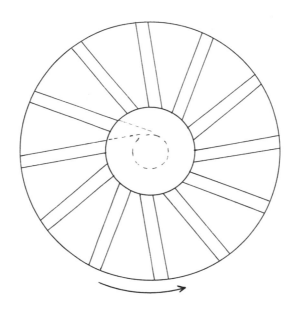

Straight Left Hand Radial Dress.
Diameter of Stone   36″
Diameter of Eye   12″
Diameter of Draft Circle   5″
Width of Furrow   1¾″

The traditional millstone dress for grain milling was frequently based on a variation of the quarter dress and sickle dress. The former comprises of a number of equal sectors or quarters each having a master furrow and a set of shorter parallel furrows. The latter has sickle shaped furrows of varying curvature, not to be mistaken with the later improved circle dress which has one or both edges of a furrow in the form of a true circular arc. These circular furrows were often marked out using a similar radius as in the size of the stone. The back edge or shoulder of the master furrows radiate tangentially from an imaginary circle drawn round the eye - called a draft circle. A grain milling rule of thumb was to provide one inch draft to each foot in diameter of the millstone, thus a four foot stone would have a four inch draft. This varied with the texture of the stone and type of dress pattern prefered. The dress is called left handed if the furrow was drawn from the draft circle to the left of the eye, and right handed, or clockwise, if drawn from the right hand side of the eye.

The older form of dress patterns had many furrows and narrow lands inbetween. By the mid 19th Century, the more enlightened millers were regarding these patterns as barbarisms. The age old art was gradually evolving into a science being forced upon the industry by economic pressures. The earlier quarter dress having few quarters of many furrows was inefficient because each furrow subsiduary to the master had a different draft circle. Since the furrow angle depends entirely upon the diameter of the draft circle, the intersecting angle of the shortest secondary furrow will be the most obtuse, and the longest secondary furrow the most acute. The principal fault of this type of dress is that the draft circle of the shortest secondary fails to fall into the grinding surface of the stone so that the grist will be drawn far out without reduction. This may not have been so apparent to the miller using larger dimension millstones that rotated relatively slow, but it would be very noticeable with the smaller, faster rotating stones which became the norm in the 19th Century. This led to the development of stones with two, at the most three, furrows per quarter, and stones having furrows of equal draft.[2]

Furrows may be circular; rectilinear, bent or spiral, and examples of all forms were present in the Flory Collection. The straight furrow dress remains the most popular and easiest to lay out. A curved dress requires more power to drive the stones than a straight one, but this is no longer the obstacle it once was when mills relied upon earlier, cruder adaptions of wind and water power. There are many forms of dress pattern with as many advantages and disadvantages to their adoption which would require several chapters to do justice to the subject. A number of different forms are depicted and described in the text to provide a sample.

---

[1]The U.S. Patent Office. (Index of patents issued from the U.S. Patent Office from 1790-1873 inclusive), pp 930-932.

[2]Prof. B. W. Dedrick, *Practical Milling,* pp. 264-267 and 281-286. Good illustration of the differing crossing angles of furrows caused by different drafts can be seen. Also discusses the path of grain in runner and under runner mills with different dress patterns.

Benjamin E. Flory (father of collector) Dressing The Runner Stone, at Flory Mill in Martic Twp., Lancaster Co., PA (1912). Note the Candlelight.

CATALOG AND SPECIFICATIONS OF STONES
MENTIONED IN THE TEXT

1) **Mortar and Pestle - Two Stones**

Mortar formed in boulder of pebble conglomerate sandstone.
Approximately 30" x 17" (76.2 cm x 43.2 cm)
Pestle naturally cylindrical of harder stone 2" x 8" long. (5.1 cm x 20.3 cm)
Total weight approximately 450 lbs. (202.5 kg)

2) **Saddlestone - Two Stones.**

Metate, concave slab of blue gray metamorphic rock. 15" x 13" (38.1 cm x
   33 cm)
Mano, eliptical cylinder flattened on grinding surface. 14" x 2" (35.6 cm x
   5.1 cm)
Use - Grinding Indian corn by Pueblo Indians
Provenance - Hopi Indian Reservation, Arizona, USA.

3) **Quern - Two Stones.**

Both Stones 23" (58.4 cm) diameter x 5½" (14 cm) (approx.) made of
   Coquina Rock.
Stand - Hollowed cypress trunk, 38" high by 27" (96.5 xm x 68.6 cm)
   diameter approx.
Weight - 400-500 lbs. (180 - 225 kg)
Use - Grinding Indian Corn by Seminole Indians.
Provenance - Florida, U.S.A.

4) **Ox Powered Crushing Mill - Two Stones.**

Base (or basin stone) one piece of limestone approx. 75" x 14" deep
   (190.5 cm x 35.6 cm)
Edge Runner, Limestone, 35" dia. x 16" wide. (88.9 cm x 90.6 cm)
Weight - Base 3,500 lbs. Runner 1,500 lbs. (1575 kg. Runner 675 kg.)
Use - Crushing grain.
Provenance - Algar Shirk Farm, West Cocalico Township, Lancaster
   County, Pennsylvania.

5) **Russian Threshing Stone - One Stone.**

Star shaped block of limestone, dimensions 23" x 30" (58.4 cm x 76.2 cm)
Weight approximately 600 lbs. (270 kg.)
Use - Threshing grain by Russian Mennonite immigrants in Kansas
   USA.

6) **Wheat Chaff Stones - Two Stones.**

Both runner and bedstone 24" dia. x 9" thick (61 cm x 22.9 cm) made from
   pebble conglomerate.
Weight - 700 lbs. (315 kg) the pair.
Use - Removing chaff from wheat after flailing or treading.
Provenance - Habecker Mill, Manor Township, Lancaster, Pennsylvania.

7) Clover Seed Hullers - Two Stones.

Both stones made of tan colored pebble conglomerate.
Under-runner 33″ dia. x 12″ deep. (83.8 cm x 30.5 cm)
Basin stone 44″ dia. x 10″ thick. (111.8 cm x 25.4 cm)
Weight - 1,850 lbs. (832.5 kg) the pair.
Use - To remove clover seed from stems after harvesting.
Provenance - Newport, Perry County, Pennsylvania, USA.

8) Buck Wheat Hullers - Two Stones.

Made from tan colored millstone grit.
33″ diameter (83.82 cm)
Use - To remove hulls or husk from buckwheat.
Provenance - McCrabb Mill, Drumore Township, Pennsylvania, U.S.A.

9) Oat Hullers - Two Stones

Both stones made from a tan pebble conglomerate and 44″ dia. by 10″
    deep (111.76 cm x 25.4 cm)
Weight - 3,200 lbs. (1440 kg) the pair.
Use - To remove shells or husks from oats to make groats.
Provenance - Near Pomeroy, Sadsbury Township, Chester County,
    Pennsylvania, USA

10) Small High Speed Mills.

(See Text)

11) Middlings and Regrinding Stones - Two Stones.

Both made from Millstone Grit and 28″ dia. x 5″ thick (71.12 cm x 12.7 cm)
Use - for regrinding wheat middlings to extract extra flour.
Provenance - Kaufman Mill, Manheim township, Lancaster County, PA.

12) Under-Runner Cone Type Stone.

Both stones made of sandstone conglomerate or millstone grit.
Under-runner approximately 48″ dia. at base tapering to 14″ dia. at top
    and 24″ high (121.92 cm x 35.6 cm x 60.96 cm)
Basin Stone - 49″ dia. at base and 29″ high (124.46 cm x 73.66 cm)
Use - Grinding grain.
Provenance - Former collection of Jacob Brooks, West Willow, Lancaster
    County, Pennsylvania.

13) Cider - Pomace Mill - Two Stones.

Trough or basin stone hewn out of solid red sandstone.
Overall diameter 67″ x 13″ deep (170.2 cm x 33cm)
Depth of interior of trough 5½″ (14 cm)
Edge Runner of limestone 52″ diameter by 12″ wide (132.1 cm x 30.5 cm)
Weight - 3,500 lbs. (1585 kg)
Use - To crush apples in cider making process.

14) Cocoa and Chocolate Mills.

a) No. 1. Nib Mill. - Two Stones.

Composition Stones from Carborundum Company, Niagara, New York.
Overall diameter 39" x 8" thick (99.1 cm x 20.3 cm); 4" abrasive thickness (10.2 cm); plus 4" concrete backing (10.2 cm)
Dress - Straight left hand furrows with circle cracking of lands.
Use - No. 1 of three tier cocoa bean reduction mills.
Provenance - Hershey Chocolate Company, Hershey, Pennsylvania.

b) No. 2 & 3 Nib Mills - Two Stones

Two horizontal millstones of pink tinted marble.
Overall diameter 40" x 7" thick (101.6 cm x 17.8 cm)
Dress - Right hand circle furrows with stitching.
Weight - 1,575 lbs. (715 kg) the pair.
Use - To reduce cocoa beans to butter in three tier mill.
Provenance - From Chocolate Factory in Lititz, Pennsylvania.

c) Chocolate Melangeur - Two Stones.

Granite chaser, or edge roller, with hexagonal cast iron axle housing sleeves.
Overall diameter 11" x 15½" long. (27.9 cm x 39.4 cm)
Use - Final mixing of chocolate syrup.
Provenance - Hershey Chocolate Co., Hershey, Pennsylvania.

15) Cork Mill

a) English - One Stone.

Horizontal bedstone of millstone grit from English Pennines.
Overall diameter 53" x 4" thick (134.6 cm x 10.2 cm)
Weight - 150 lbs. (67.5 kg)
Dress - Right hand radial dress with deep bosum.
Use - Fine finish grinding of corkwood.
Provenance - Armstrong Cork Company, Lancaster, Pennsylvania

b) American - One Stone

Runner stone of millstone grit from Indiana County, Pennsylvania
Overall diameter 54" x 20½" thick (137.2 cm x 52.1 cm)
Weight - Approx. 3,500 lbs. (1589 kg)
Dress, Use, and Provenance as in "a" above

16) Dye Mill - Two Stones

Hand Quern of grey granite.
Overall diameter 26" x 7½ deep (66.1 cm x 19.1 cm)
Weight - 400 lbs. (181 kg)
Use - To grind dye stuffs for wool dyeing.
Provenance - Woolen Mill in Lancaster County, Pennsylvania.

17) **Flint Mill - Four Stones**

Bed or basin stone of grey granite.
Overall diameter 72″ x 19″ thick (182.9 cm x 48.3 cm)
Two granite edge runners 42″ overall diameter x 24″ wide overall
  diameter (106.7 cm x 61 cm)
One smaller granite edge runner 19″ x 24″ overall diameter
  (48.3 cm x 61 cm)
Weights - Base 7,900 lbs (3555 kg); Edge Runners 3,800 lbs. each (1710 kg);
  Smaller runner 400 lbs. (180 kg)
Use - To grind flint powder for ceramics.
Provenance - Baird Flint Mill, in York County, Pennsylvania.

18) **Gypsum Mill - Two Stones**

Both stones of tan colored conglomerate.
Overall diameter stationary 58″ x 19″ deep (147.3 cm x 48.3 cm);
  Under runner 36″ x 23″ deep (91.4 cm x 58.4 cm).
Weight - 3,700 lbs. (1665 kg) the pair.
Use - To grind gypsum for land plaster (fertilizer).
Provenance - Wagners Mill, Perry County, Pennsylvania.

19) **Hemp Mill - One Stone.**

Tapered edge roller of sandstone. (117.8 cm x 44.5 cm).
Overall diameter widest end 44″ x 17½″ (117.8 cm x 44.5 cm) diameter
  small end.
Total length 29½″ (74.9 cm).
Weight - approx. 1,000 lbs. (450 kg).
Use - To break hemp plant stems to separate fibers.
Provenance Old Frey Mill, McCall Ferry, York County, Pennsylvania

20) **Phosphate Mill - Two Stones.**

Composite Stones, granite bosum, carborundum skirt.
Overall diameter 36″ x 7″ (91.4 cm x 17.8 cm).
Dress - Left hand furrow radial with traces of sickle dress feathering or
  stitching.
Use - To grind phosphate rock in manufacture of fertilizers.
Provenance - Chas. Ross and Company, Brooklyn, New York.

21) **Tanbark Mill - One Stone.**

Edge runner stone of grey conglomerate.
Overall diameter 45″ x 13″ wide (114.3 x 33 cm)
Weight - 1,500 lbs. (675 kg)
Use - To crush bark for use in tannery.
Provenance - Tannery Site, Near Cocalico Township, Lancaster Co.
  Pennsylvania.

22) Paint and Color Mills

a) Revolving Bed Chaser or Pan Mill.
Esopus bed stone 4'6" diameter. (137.2 cm).
Two rollers or chasers 36" x 14" face. (91.4 cm x 35.6 cm).
Weight of total mill on skids 9,950 lbs. (4477.5 kg).
Use - Heavy crushing of materials in dry or semi-dry state.
Provenance - Charles Ross & Son, Brooklyn, New York.

b) Double Eccentric Tub or Enamel Mill.

Esopus stone and granite bed stones used.
Sizes built 20, 30, 36, 42, and 54 inch (50.8 cm, 76.2 cm, 91.4, 106.7 cm,
137.2 cm) diameter bed stones.
Use - For grinding materials extremely fine in water.
Provenance - Charles Ross & Son, Brooklyn, New York.

c) Horizontal Under-runner Mill.

Esopus millstones of 20, 26, 30 and 36 inch (50.8 cm, 66 cm,
76.2 cm, 91.4 cm) diameter.
Use - For lead and heavy paste grinding.
Provenance - Charles Ross & Son, Brooklyn, New York.

GLOSSARY

ATTRITION   Abrasion; the wearing away by friction or by rubbing substances together.

BED CHASER   See Pan Mill.

BED STONE   Lower fixed millstone of a horizontal pair.

BEETLING   In cloth manufacture; the beating or pounding process in the manufacture of linen by an implement (beetle) consisting of a heavy head usually wood with a handle or stock.

BOSUM   The area of a millstone's grinding face surrounding the eye - the inner portion of the face, usually concave to varing degrees.

BRIDGETREE   An adjustable beam supporting the thrust bearing below a stone spindle; it can be raised or lowered to adjust the gap between the grinding faces of a millstone.

CALCINED FLINT   Flint nodules roasted in a kiln to make them easier to crush.

CHERT   A variety of quartz, resembling flint, but more brittle, occurring in strata; also called hornstone.

CONGLOMERATE STONE   A rock composed of rounded fragments of various rocks cemented together in a mass of hardened clay and sand.

COQUINA ROCK   A soft, whitish rock of recent formation in the West Indies and Florida; made up of fragments of marine shells united by a calcareous cement.

CORDUROY BED   Composed of logs laid closely side by side giving a ribbed surface resembling corduroy cloth.

CORN   Used in American context to denote only maize (Indian corn) and not as a collective term for various grains as in Britain.

CRACKING   The fine lines or grooves cut in the lands of a dressed millstone. Same as stitching.

CULLIN STONE   German millstone of blue/black lava distributed from Cologne. Same as Blue or Dutch Stone.

CUSTOM MILL   A mill that grinds grain for customers in return for a toll or portion of the end product.

DAMSEL   An iron or wooden rod terminating in a fork or crutch which straddles the rynd on an under driven runner stone. It agitates the shoe feeding grain to the stones.

DRESS   The pattern of furrows cut into the grinding face of a millstone, also the procedure of sharpening the millstones.

> **Circular Dress**   Has furrows which have one or both edges cut in a true circular arc.

> **Logrithmic Dress**   The furrows are generally all alike in length as well as in curvature and the crossing angles of the furrows are constant all the way out.

> **Quarter Dress**   Type of dressing which divides the grinding surface of a millstone into regions called quarters, or Harps, each quarter having a master furrow and one or more subsidiary furrows.

> **Sickle Dress**   Having curved furrows of varying curvature similar but not to be confused with circular dress.

DUTCH FAN   Mechanical fan with revolving blades for winnowing grain.

EDGE RUNNER   Stones designed to rotate in a vertical plane, the edge forming the crushing surfaces.

EXHAUSTING OF MILLSTONES   Drawing off of dust from rotating millstones within an enclosed duct to prevent a build up of combustible dust which could be ignited by friction of the millstones.

EYE   The hole in the center of the runner stone.

FEATHERING   See stitching. (Feathering is the American term.)

FLAIL   An instrument for threshing grain by hand consisting of a wooden staff or handle at the end of which a stouter and shorter pole or club called a swingle or swipple is hung as to swing freely.

FLAX BRAKE   A machine for removing the woody and cellular portion of flax from the fibrous portion. The hemp-brake is substantially similar in its construction and identical in its purpose.

FRENCH BURR   Millstone made up of shaped blocks of a freshwater quartz quarried in the Paris Basin, France, and renowned for wheat-flour production.

FURROWS   Grooves or channels cut into the grinding face of a millstone.

GIN   Machine by which gears or machinery is operated by draft animal walking round in a circle.

GRISTMILL   A grain grinding mill. Syn. with Custom Mill.

HARDINGE MILL   A tricone type of ball mill; the cones become steeper from the feed end towards the discharge end.

HARP   Segment of the grinding face of a millstone, containing regular pattern of land and furrows. Syn. with Quarters.

HECKLE   (Hackle)   An instrument set with parallel steel pins for splitting and combing out the fibers of flax or hemp - a flax comb.

HIGH GRINDING   Grinding with the millstones widely separated necessitating a number of regrinds.

HOMINY Foodstuff made from hulled and coarsely broken maize (corn) mixed with water and boiled; hulled maize.

HULLING STONES Millstones which remove the outer husks including the bran of cereal grains.

HURST FRAME (Synonymous with Husk Frame) Timber or metal framework carrying the millstones and enclosing the main transmission or gear train in a watermill when the stones are driven from beneath.

LANDS Grinding surface of a millstone between the furrows.

MEERSCHAUM Soft white claylike heat resistant mineral, a hydrous magnesium silicate used for tobacco pipes etc.

MILLSTONE GRIT A coarse, quartz-like, sandstone which has been used for millstones. Found at stratum below coal measures (seams); member of carboniferous group.

NEW PROCESS MILLING The process of high grinding, with one or more lower regrinds, that came into use in the United States just before the introduction of roller milling.

PAN MILL Mill comprising of a metal, stone or wood, pan in which turn one or more edge runners to crush material; usually associated with wet grinding.

PONY STONE In new process milling, the smaller pair of millstones that were sometimes used to grind the middlings.

PRITCHELL A pointed punch or pick of tempered steel used in the dressing of millstones.

PURIFIER A machine in which an air current blown up through middlings vibrating on an oscillating sieve is used to separate them from the free bran with which they are associated. The middlings are then ready for a finer grind.

QUARTER DRESS See "Dress".

QUANT The driving spindle, normally of iron, used to rotate over driven millstones.

RETTING Of hemp and flax; the process or preparing for the separation of the woody parts of the stems of the plants from the filamentous parts by soaking them in water or by exposure to dew.

ROLLER MILL Mill employing a number of pairs of facing rollers to break and reduce the grain.

RUNNER STONE The upper revolving millstone of a horizontal pair.

RYND The metal crosspiece fixed in the eye of a runner stone by which it is carried on top of the stone spindle which allows it to rotate freely above the lower (bed) stone.

> **Balance Rynd** Two armed, allows the runner stone to pivot and balance above the stone spindle; replaced the earlier fixed rynd.

> **Fixed Rynd** Usually four, sometimes three, armed, withheld the runner stone firmly in a plane parallel to the lower stone.

SICKLE DRESS See "Dress".

SILICOSIS   A chronic lung disease caused by continued inhalation of silica dust.

SKIRT   The outer portion of the grinding face of a millstone.

SLAB AND MULLER   Flat stone on which material is reduced by a hand held stone rubbed or rolled above it.

SORGHUM   A tall plant somewhat similar in appearance to maize. Sweet sorghum varieties yield syrups and molasses from the boiled cane juice, also grown for forage, silage and feed grains.

STAMP MILL   Mill in which material held in a mortar, is pulverized or reduced by being continually pounded by a heavy weight secured to the lower end of a vertical shaft.

STITCHING   See "Cracking".

STONE SPINDLE   The iron spindle which carries the runner millstone and also drives it in the case of under driven stones.

TANNIN   Tannic acid. An astringent liquid derived from oak bark gallnuts, etc. and used in tanning, dyeing, etc.

TENTERING   Adjusting the distance between the two millstones.

THRESHING DRUM   A machine to separate out grain from the straw and husk.

TRAMMING   The task of aligning the stone spindle to turn vertically through the bedstone bush after leveling the bedstone.

UNDER RUNNER   A lower revolving millstone of a horizontal pair.

VAT   Synonym for stone casing and tun. Wooden or metal case enclosing a pair of millstones.

VIBROENERGY SEPARATOR   A screen type device for separation of grains of solids by a combination of gyratory motion and auxilliary vibration caused by balls bouncing against the lower surface of the screen cloth.

WHITING MILL   A mill to crush chalk and lime to make a white wash or form of paint.

WINNOWER   Large shallow basket held or shaken in the wind to blow chaff and other light refuse material from the threshed grain.

WINNOWING FAN   Fan which blows chaff, dust etc. from uncleaned grains as it passes through a "box" and sieve.

BIBLIOGRAPHY

Books

Appleton. *Dictionary of Machines, Mechanics and Engine Work and Engineering.* Vol. II. London, 1852.

Arch, Fredric Blakey. *The Florida Phosphate Industry.* Cambridge, Massachusetts: Harvard University Press, 1973.

Barlow, P. *Manufacturers and Machinery of Great Britain.* London: Baldwin and Cradock, 1836.

Bathe, Greville and Dorothy. *Oliver Evans, A Chronicle of Early American Engineering.* Philadelphia, 1935.

Bennett, R. and Elton, John. *History of Cornmilling.* (4 Volumes)
Vol. I   *Handstones, Slave and Cattle Mills   1898.*
Vol. II   *Watermills and Windmills*   1899.
Vol. III   *Feudal Laws and Customs*   1900.
Vol. IV   *Some Feudal Mills*   1904.
London: Simpkin Marshall and Company.

Betts, Edwin Morris, ed. *Thomas Jefferson's Farm Book.* University Press of Virginia, 1976.

Bishop, J. Leander. *A History of American Manufacturers from 1606 to 1860.* Philadelphia, 1868.

Bivins, John Jr. *The Moravian Potters at Old Salem North Carolina.* University of North Carolina Press, 1972.

Bockler, G. A. *Theatrum Machinarum Novum.* 1622.

Chambers, E. *Universal Dictionary of Arts and Sciences.* London, 1781.

Clark, Victor S. *History of Manufacturers in the United States.* New York: McGraw Hill Book Company, 1929.

Copeland, Robert. *A Short History of Pottery, Raw Materials and the Cheddleton Flint Mill.* Henley on Trent U.K.: Cheddleton Flint Mill Industrial Trust, 1972.

Craik, David. *Practical American Millwright and Miller.* Philadelphia, 1870.

Dedrick, Prof. B. W. *Practical Milling.* Chicago, Illinois: National Miller, 1924.

Derry, T. K. and Williams, T. I. *A Short History of Technology.* Oxford, 1960.

Evans, Oliver. *The Young Millwright and Millers Guide. 13th Edition, 1850. New York: Reprinted by Arno Press, 1972.*

Ferguson, Eugene S. *Oliver Evans.* Wilmington, Delaware: Hagley Museum, 1980.

Gregory, G. *Dictionary of Arts and Sciences.* New York, 1821.

Grinding and Crushing. A Bibliography. London: H. M. Stationary Office, 1958.

Hommel, Rudolf P. *China at Work*. Massachusetts Institute of Technology, 1937. (Reprinted 1969)

Hughes, William Carter. *The American Miller and Millwrights Assistant*. Philadelphia, 1884.

Hunter, Louis C. *Waterpower, A History of Industrial Power in the United States, 1780-1930*. University of Virginia Press, 1979.

Knight, E. H. *American Mechanical Dictionary*. Vol. III. Boston, 1876.

Morfit, Cambell. *The Arts of Tanning, Currying and Leather Dressing*. English translation of French Classic by De Fontenelle J. and Malpeyre, F. Philadelphia, 1852.

Moritz, L. A. *Grain Mills and Flour in Classical Antiquity*. Oxford: Clarendon Press, 1958.

Mountfor, A. R. *Illustrated Guide to Staffordshire Salt Glazed Stoneware*. London, 1971.

Proulx and Nichols, *Sweet and Hard Cider*. Charlotte, Vermont: Garden Way Publishing Inc., 1980.

Quick, Graeme R. and Buchele, Wesley, F. *The Grain Harvesters*. American Society of Agricultural Engineers. 1978.

Rees, Abraham. *Cyclopeadia of Arts and Sciences and Literature*. Kibdib, 1819.

Schlebecker, John T. *Whereby We Thrive*. Iowa State University Press, 1975.

Severin, Tim. *The Brendan Voyage*. New York: McGraw Hill Book Co., 1978.

Storck, John & Teaque, Walter Darvin. *Flour for Man's Bread*. Minneapolis: University of Minnesota Press, 1952.

Vrest, Orton. *The American Cider Book*. New York: Farar Straus and Giroux, 1973.

Weatherwax, Paul. *Indian Corn in Old America*. New York: McMillan Co., 1954.

Weiss, Harry B. and Ziegler, Grace M. *Forgotten Mills of Early New Jersey*. Trenton, New Jersey: New Jersey Agricultural Society, 1960.

Weiss, Harry B. *History of Tanning In New Jersey:* Trenton, New Jersey: New Jersey Agricultural Society.

Werne. *Source of the White Nile*. London, 1841.

Papers

Anderson, Russell H. "Technical Ancestry of Grain Milling Devices," *Agricultural History,* Vol 12 (July, 1938), 256-270.

Birnson, M. "John Dwight." *Transaction of English Ceramic Circle*. Vol. 5, part 2, (1961), 95-109.

Butowski, A. "The Means of Improving the Management Cultivation and Fabrication of Hemp," St. Petersburg, Russia, 1842. English translation by Von Smidt, P. in the *New American State Papers, Agriculture,* Vol. 2, Wilmington, 1973.

Flory, Paul B. "Old Millstones." Paper read before the Lancaster County Historical Society, Lancaster Pennsylvania, Vo. LV. No. 3, 1951.

Kirk, Calib. *American Farmer.* Articles on clover mills in Vol. II No. 42 (January 12, 1821), 335-336. Vol. III No. 45 (February 2, 1821) 357-358.

Litchfield, Dr. Carter. "Early Pennsylvania Hemp Mills." Transaction of the *International Molinological Society,* Vol. 5, 1983.

Pieters, A. J. "Seed Selling, Seed Growing and Seed Testing." (Improvements in harvesting and cleaning grass and clover seeds, pp. 565-566), *1899 Yearbook of U.S. Department of Agriculture,* 1900, pp. 549-574.

Quisenberry, K. S. and Heitz. L. P. "Turkey Wheat: The Cornerstone of an Empire," Read before the Symposium--Farming in the Mid West, 1840-1900. *Agricultural History Journal* of the Agricultural History Society, Vol. XLVIII, No. 1 (January, 1974).

Radley, Jeffrey, M. A. "Millstones and Hallamshire Grindstones." Excerpts of transactions of the *Newcomen Society* Vol. XXXVI, 1963-4.

Todd, S. Edward. "Improved Farm Implements." Report of the Commissioner of Agriculture (1866), 225-288.

Webb, William S. "Old Millstones of Kentucky." *Filson Club History Quarterly* Vol. 9 No. 4 Louisville, Kentucky (October, 1935).

Pamphlets

Armstrong Cork Co. *Cork Its Origins and Many Uses.* Lancaster, Pennsylvania, 1930.